The Rich and the Poor

The Rich and the Poor

A Christian Perspective on Global Economics

CARL KREIDER

HERALD PRESS
Scottdale, Pennsylvania
Kitchener, Ontario
1987

Library of Congress Cataloging-in-Publication Data
Kreider, Carl, 1914-
    The rich and the poor.

    Bibliography: p.
    1. Economics—Moral and ethical aspects.
2. Capitalism—Moral and ethical aspects.
3. Developing countries—Economic conditions.
4. Developing countries—Economic policy.   I. Title.
HB72.K74   1987   261.8'5   86-33614
ISBN 0-8361-3433-8 (pbk.)

To Andrew, Rachel, and Eleanor—

Children from rich countries whose lives will be greatly affected by the way affluent societies respond to the needs of the poor

Contents

Preface 11
Introduction 15

1. How Poor Are the Poor Countries? 25

2. What Are Poor Countries Like? 36

3. Reducing the Rate of Population Growth 53

4. Agricultural and Rural Development 69

5. Human Development: Education and Health 88

6. Stimulating Industrial Development 105

7. International Cooperation 121

8. What Can I Do? 139

Suggestions for Further Reading 155
Index 157
The Author 167

If any of you have the world's goods
and see another in need,
yet close your heart against that person,
how can God's love abide in you?
Little children,
let us not love in word or speech
but in deed and in truth.
(1 John 3:17-18, paraphrased)

Preface

I was stimulated to write this book by the appearance of an excellent book, *The Economics of Developing Countries* by E. Wayne Nafziger, a former student of mine. His book should enjoy wide sales as it is used for college-level courses in economic development. However, I felt that there was a need for a book which would treat some of the same material more briefly and less technically.

I hope that this book will be of interest to the general reader. An increasing number of thoughtful people are deeply disturbed by the poverty of the vast majority of peoples of the world. They may not have the time to read a long and detailed book. I am thinking especially of many people who are now traveling to parts of the world beyond the "grand tour" of Europe. As they go to the countries of Central and South America—and perhaps of Africa and Asia as well—Christian tourists should not be satisfied to stay in the expensive hotels in the major cities and gain only the most superficial knowledge of the country being visited. The tourist hotels in Nairobi and Buenos Aires are not much different from those in Columbus, Ohio, or Atlanta, Georgia. Can't a Christian, in making a trip to Less Developed Countries (LDCs), decide that the purpose of the trip is not just to pity the poor but to try to understand them and think deeply about what needs to be done to improve their lot?

I also intend that this book will be used by discussion groups of church people. With them in mind I have added a small list of discussion questions at the end of each chapter. These questions are designed to lead to other more profound ones which will emerge from the discussion groups themselves.

For the past 12 years I have been teaching a course in comparative economic systems. In this course I have tried to help students think through the differences between the economies of capitalist countries, countries of the Eastern bloc ("communist" countries), and countries of the third world, often called Less Developed Countries (LDCs). I have found the *World Development Reports*, published annually since 1978 by the World Bank, to be especially helpful in understanding the unique situation and problems of the LDCs. My students have at times found them to be rather tough reading. In writing this book I have drawn much from them, and I hope that I have simplified the issues they discuss.

I make reference to the *World Development Reports* in each of the first five chapters of this book. This should not be interpreted as meaning that these reports were the only source of my information for these chapters. I have drawn from many other sources as well.

The usual way for scholars to express this dependence is to use footnotes. Inasmuch as I have written this book for the general public rather than the scholarly community, I have made a conscious decision to limit my use of footnotes. Similarly I have decided to use statistical tables only sparingly. I realize that some readers find tables helpful. But I know that others are intimidated or burdened by them.

The reader of this book will quickly discover that I write from a capitalist bias. I am quite aware that all economic systems stand under the judgment of God. Most economists (even the critics of capitalism) recognize the accomplishments of the capitalist system in the production of goods and services. The critics of capitalism fault it for the inequities in the distribution of wealth and income which have accompanied the amazing expansion in production. I recognize this as a grievous fault.

But economic development will be delayed and perhaps aborted unless production is increased. I believe that capitalist methods offer the most promise of increasing production. I think it is incumbent upon Christians to use the resources available to them from superior production methods to enhance the standard of living of the world's poor. This book is designed to be at least a modest contribution toward that end. At the same time, I am aware that my capitalist bias may be offensive to those who find a socialist perspective more attractive. To such I offer my apologies.

I write this book as a Christian economist. I realize that some would consider this a contradiction in terms. I must respectfully disagree. But I am a Christian first, an economist second.

The rough draft of this book was written during the spring, summer, and fall of 1985, after I had retired from teaching at Goshen College. The rough draft was read by four of my former students. E. Wayne Nafziger is now a professor of development economics at Kansas State University and a frequent visitor to LDCs as he seeks to engage in research on their development problems. Melvin J. Loewen lived for a number of years in Zaire. He is now Senior Operations Officer and Regional Coordinator of the Economic Development Institute of the World Bank. Although his office is in Washington, D.C., his work involves frequent and extensive travel in LDCs.

Randal Gunden, recently appointed to the economics faculty at Goshen College, teaches courses in development economics. In the winter trimester of 1986 he used a preliminary draft of this book for one of his classes. Gunden served for a period of three years in two developing countries of Africa.

My oldest son, Alan F. Kreider at the London Mennonite Centre, though not a specialist in this subject, is a former student of mine as well. Since he has the ability to write clearly, I appreciate his insistence that I should do the same.

There is an old saying that "a stream cannot rise above its source." The laws of physics support this statement. But if students were not able to rise above their teachers, the progress of knowledge would long since have been stopped. These former students of mine clearly have risen above their teacher. For this I am grateful to God. There is no greater satisfaction to a teacher than that which stems from the knowledge that what he tried to do (albeit imperfectly), others are carrying on with greater skill.

I have profited much from the incisive comments made by these persons who have read with care the rough draft of this book. I did not always accept their advice, and so I must accept the final responsibility for the book's errors of fact or of judgment.

My wife, Evelyn, had hoped that when I retired from teaching, I would lead a more relaxed life. I am afraid that my writing of this book, among other things, has dashed this hope. She not only accepted it without a whimper; she encouraged me at every step. I can't thank her adequately for this or for her many other gifts to me through all the years of our life together.

—Carl Kreider
Goshen, Indiana

Introduction

Some people are rich. Some people are poor. No one who has had occasion to travel by car from Westchester County, New York, to Appalachia needs to be reminded of this.

But when one travels abroad, one soon becomes conscious that some *countries* are rich and some are poor. India is a poor country. Thus when one gets off the plane in Calcutta on a night in June and takes a taxi to a hotel in the center of the city, one sees people sleeping in the streets with scarcely any visible possessions. If the next day one takes a short trip to a village beyond the suburbs, one will find that the people there have no electricity and no running water. There is no glass in the windows of the houses and scarcely any furniture inside. The floors are packed dirt. Countries like India are usually referred to today as Less Developed Countries, or LDCs.

What do these sharp differences mean to people with sensitive Christian consciences? What do they mean to genuine fellowship within the Christian church? The apostle James was concerned about this problem nearly 2000 years ago. He wrote:

> My brethren, show no partiality. ... For if a man with gold rings and in fine clothing comes into your assembly, and a poor man with shabby clothing also comes in, and you pay attention to the one who wears fine clothing and say, "Have a seat here, please," while you say to the poor man, "Stand there," or "Sit at my feet," have you not made distinction among yourselves, and become judges with evil thoughts? ... But if you show partiality, you commit sin, and are convicted by the law as transgressors. (James 2:1-4, 9)

James was thinking of a problem in a particular congregational situation, but he was no doubt aware that there were many congregations during his time where this kind of invidious comparison between the rich and the poor was evident. But when we think of the Christian church today, we think of an institution which—far from being confined to a small area in the Middle East—has assemblies in all continents. Each congregation in whatever continent no doubt has worshipers who are richer and poorer. But in some parts of the world the poorest people attending a Christian church service have a standard of living which is higher than that enjoyed by the richest in other parts of the world. This arises because some people live in developed countries and other people live in LDCs.

Menno Simons, an articulate leader of the Radical Reformation in the Netherlands and North Germany in the sixteenth century, would have been shocked by differences in the standards of living within the church of Christ. To be sure, they existed in the Roman Catholic Church and in the establishment churches which resulted from the Reformation. But Menno viewed it as a sign of the true church that there were no poor among them. For nearly 200 years missionaries have gone from rich countries of Europe and North America to the countries of Asia, Africa, and Latin America. They have brought with them the good news which the sending churches celebrate as they worship in comfortable meetinghouses. Occasionally "fraternal" delegates from third world churches are brought to Europe and North America. International conferences of Christians seek to promote Christian fellowship across the lines of nation and of continent.

But can there be real fellowship between rich people from churches in wealthy countries and poor people from churches in LDCs? Or is there the kind of "partiality" that James noted? And if so, is this what James called "sin"? And are the people who engage in it "transgressors"?

This book is written with the conviction that although thoughtful people are generally somewhat aware of the differences in standards of living between rich countries and poor countries, we could all be more faithful followers of Christ if our awareness were heightened. Our news media keep us constantly aware of the unrest in the poorer sections of the world. Often it leaves us with the impression that most of this unrest is Marxist in origin and is directed by the Soviet Union. When Christian thinkers from the LDCs talk about "liberation theology," some Christians in rich countries are troubled by it because they think that it, too, is Marxist-inspired rather than Christian. Is there a chance that the rich can understand the poor? I am not sure, but I hope that this book will make at least a small contribution to a better understanding.

Such a better understanding has many facets, but the focus of this book is on the economic elements of it. Although it has been my privilege to travel on every continent and to have spent a year in one of the world's poorest countries (Ethiopia), I do not claim to qualify as an expert on economic development. Instead I have drawn on the experiences and writings of others who have made far more scientific studies of the problem than I have.

This book therefore will not represent an advance in technical economics. Its purpose is to treat the problem in simple language. And I hope that it will lead to vigorous discussion of the issues raised and to intelligent action in response to these issues.

Some of the terms which I will use may be new to some of my readers. Gross National Product (GNP), infrastructure, subsistence production, import substitution—these and other terms frequently used by development economists are, I find, unavoidable. But when I use them I will first define them in nontechnical language.

I will begin in chapter 1 with an attempt to answer the question of just how poor the poor nations actually are. GNP is the most commonly used measure of poverty or affluence, but it is a defective one. What are the problems in determining GNP (especially for poor nations)? What are the problems of inter-country comparisons?

In chapter 2 I will move on to a description of some of the main characteristics of the poor countries. Chapters 3 to 7 are the heart of the book. In them I will discuss some of the things which can be done to raise the standard of living of the poor countries, such as reducing the rate of population growth, expanding agricultural production, improving educational and health facilities, stimulating the growth of manufacturing, and providing for better international cooperation.

Chapter 8 makes all these issues personal: 'What can I do?" I wish the chapter were longer. I will be delighted if readers will add their own suggestions to mine.

In writing these pages I will not often pause to ask, "Now what will the Christian do about this?" Rather, I will depend on Christian consciences which are already sensitized but which can, if better informed, develop more creative responses. It is my conviction that the church is always led by the Spirit, but that the Spirit asks for our cooperation in carrying out God's holy will. Furthermore, I believe that there is no single issue which hampers the work of the Spirit more than the sharp differences in the standards of living which we have permitted to develop. How often we defend these differences with arguments which in the final analysis are really lame!

Possible solutions to the problems of development are so complex that it should not be surprising if there were differences of opinion concerning the best steps which should be taken to solve them.

I want to avoid two extreme positions. Some have held that the poor countries are victims of forces over which they have no control. I will observe in chapter 2 that most of the LDCs were formerly colonies of some great world power. When they achieved their independence they did not immediately become rich. Instead they suffered with "economic colonialism." Some would say that their poverty was caused entirely by others. If this is the case, the only effective way to improve the lot of the poor nations is to get other nations to change their policies.

At the other extreme are people who say that the poverty of the poor countries is entirely their own fault. If this is the case, the only way to improve would be for poor countries to put their own houses in order.

I believe that the answer lies somewhere between these two

extreme positions. I think that the rich countries can change their policies in ways which would benefit the poor countries. In subsequent chapters I plan to suggest some of these. But I am also convinced that the poor nations will need to make changes which will enable them to help themselves. Jesse Jackson, referring to the poor in the United States, is reported to have declared: "You can't lift yourselves by your own bootstraps if you don't have boots." Rich countries must supply the boots, but poor countries must do the lifting.

Regardless of where the fault lies, the basic task of economic development is this—enhancing the level of production in the poor countries. But the poorest people who live in LDCs will not benefit from increased production unless attention is also given to more equitable distribution of the larger total product. Therefore, both higher production and more equitable distribution, are needed.

Production results from a combination of the various factors of production: land, labor, capital, and entrepreneurship (management). "Land" here consists of the all of the God-given natural resources of a country. This includes farmland, of course, but it also includes rivers and natural harbors and such climatic factors as an adequate rainfall and growing season. Mineral resources such as oil have made some countries very rich. Coal and iron in abundance have contributed to the economic development of the United States and some of the countries of Western Europe.

Labor represents the human element in production. It must be adequate in amount, but can there be too many people? Population policy will be included in our study.

Workers need to be trained. We will need to examine the relation of education to economic development and the reduction of poverty.

To achieve maximum production, workers must be healthy. How can levels of health be raised?

Capital consists of "produced means of production." We will see that this is far broader than factories and machinery. It also includes roads, schools, hospitals—and transportation and communication equipment.

An important consideration is that capital must always be the result of saving. The saving need not be done in the country where the capital is being used. It may result from borrowing from other countries or from international agencies. From what sources can capital be accumulated and how can it be used most effectively in production?

The fourth factor—entrepreneurship—refers to the organization of the other three factors for maximum production. This is one of the major services which business people render. It involves both skill in management and the willingness to take risks. Many of the poorer countries suffer from a lack in this important part of production. The growth of capitalism in the West has been attributed by some to the "Protestant ethic" of hard work. How can an entrepreneurial spirit be engendered in LDCs?

Production is a result of the combination of all of these factors. The United States and Canada have become prosperous because they are richly endowed with all four factors. But Japan has shown that it can become one of the most rapidly growing and now one of the world's richest countries even though it is certainly not rich in natural resources.

Some ill-informed people have charged that poor countries are poor because their workers do not work hard; they have not adopted the "Protestant work ethic." Anyone who is tempted to this simplistic explanation of poverty should observe people from poor countries at work. In 1956 our family took a boat trip from Japan to Europe. The ship carried both cargo and passengers. We stopped at the (then) French port of Djibouti, at the foot of the Red Sea. I observed African stevedores unloading cargo from the hold of the ship. It was a blisteringly hot day in that equatorial climate. I perspired freely as I stood in a gentle breeze watching the workers. The ship had a rigid schedule to maintain, forcing the workers to work at top speed. There was no air-conditioning in the hold of the ship and no natural ventilation. I have never seen workers anywhere work so hard. But in spite of their near-superhuman efforts, these workers were poorly paid.

The individual business firm uses capital. But development

economists also use the term *capital* more broadly when they refer to "infrastructure." A term with similar meaning is "social overhead capital." Whichever term one prefers, infrastructure may be divided between physical infrastructure and institutional infrastructure. The physical includes roads, harbors, transportation and communication equipment, schools, hospitals, and other health facilities. Electric power facilities will also be needed. They will come first to the cities, where they will not only produce higher living standards for the people, but will also provide for the growing needs of factories.

The institutional infrastructure includes many items which people in developed countries take for granted. There should be a banking system and other financial intermediaries. Laws must be developed which will provide for the protection of property rights and the enforcement of contracts. In some cases, the development of these institutions may seem to nullify long-standing cultural values. Some cultures, for example, have religious prohibitions against the paying of interest. Sometimes decisions will need to be made between slowing the pace of economic development and maintaining some of these long-standing cultural values.

Having made these preliminary observations, we are now in a position to begin our study of economic development.

The Rich and the Poor

1

How Poor
Are the Poor Countries?

Gross National Product

We think of the poverty or affluence of a people measured either by the income they earn or by the amount of property they have accumulated. The most frequently used measure of a country's income is its Gross National Product (GNP). This aggregate figure is then divided by the population to get the *per capita* GNP. For the United States this figure in 1984 was $15,390. For Bangladesh it was only $130. This is an enormous disparity. But does it really mean that the average person in the United States is 118 times as well off as the average citizen of Bangladesh?

Before we can answer this question, we should pause to see how GNP is calculated. Then we will be able to understand some of the weaknesses in using per capita GNP as the sole measure of wealth or poverty.

Economists use a simple mathematical equation to define GNP. It is as follows:

$$GNP = C + I + G$$

In this equation, "C" is the total amount of consumer expenditures for goods and services. These expenditures do not need to be made in money, although in a highly developed economy most of them are monetary. "I" is investment expenditures. Economists use the term *investment* in a way which differs from popular speech. To the layperson, investment may consist of buying stocks or bonds on the securities exchanges. But the economist thinks of investment as "capital formation."

We have already noted that capital consists of manufactured goods which are used to produce other goods. This means that a business person's construction or purchase of a new factory building (or of the machinery which the building contains) is an investment. So also retailers are investing when they add to their inventories. Similarly farmers are investing by increasing their herds of dairy cattle, by building barns, or by draining the swampy parts of their land.

The "G" in the equation simply represents total government expenditures for goods and services. This includes state and local governmental units as well as federal.

It should be emphasized that the economist (in his or her role as an economist) attaches no moral judgment to the intrinsic worth of any of these expenditures. A country is not necessarily better morally because it has a larger GNP. Harmful things like beverage alcohol and smoking tobacco count as a part of consumer expenditures in GNP just as much as an expenditure of similar size for baby food. The purchase of a new still for a liquor factory counts as an investment expenditure just as much as the purchase of new ovens for a bakery. Government purchases of military hardware and superfluous atomic weaponry count as much toward GNP as government purchases of similar size for new highways, hospitals, or schools.

A crude illustration may help clarify these points. Let us assume that a playboy has been given an expensive new car by his father. He drinks too much alcohol, drives his car while intoxicated, and gets in a bad accident, demolishing the car of the other driver (as well as his own new one). Both drivers are permanently disabled quadraplegics as a result of the accident. But his indulgent father buys him a new car and hires a driver to drive it for the son. The whole episode has resulted in large expenditures for hospital and medical bills and for the purchase of new cars. This increases GNP, but no one would say that welfare of the son, his unfortunate victim, or of the country in which they live has been enhanced.

Today practically every country, even quite small and poor ones, publishes figures for its GNP. These figures are most readily available in the *World Development Reports*, which have been published annually since 1978 for the World Bank by the Oxford University Press. The most recent of these reports provides nearly 170 pages of text discussing material pertinent to economic development. It also contains over 70 pages of statistical tables. It is not necessary for me to reprint these tables in this book. Instead, from time to time I plan to give some pertinent facts from them. Readers who are interested in more detail can get the reports themselves from any good college or university library or from most of the larger public libraries.

The per capita GNP figures which I cited in the first paragraph of this chapter were taken from the tables on pages 180 and 181 of the *World Development Report 1986*. On these pages are similar figures for 120 countries which are members of the World Bank. These countries are divided into six categories and the average GNP for each group of countries is given as well as the specific figure for each country individually.

The following table is a selection of 28 countries from this list. To simplify the table I have included in it only those countries which have populations of over 30 million people. Saudi Arabia is the only exception to this rule. I have included it because it is the largest of the high-income oil exporters.

The poorest on the list are 36 countries called low-income economies. Their annual GNP ranges from only $110 per capita for Ethiopia to $380 for Pakistan. The average for the whole group is only $260. The middle-income economies are divided into two parts: 40 lower-middle-income countries with an average GNP per person of $740 and 20 upper-middle-income countries with an average per capita GNP of $1950. The next group consists of five countries called high-income oil exporters. Some of these countries now have larger per capita GNPs than the highly developed countries of Western Europe, Japan, and North America. Saudi Arabia is the most populous of these countries, but even Saudi Arabia has only 11 million inhabitants. Its average GNP is $10,530.

Low Income Economies

	Population (millions) 1984	*Per capita GNP (dollars)*	*Life expectancy at birth (years) 1984*
Ethiopia	42.2	110	44
Bangladesh	98.1	130	50
Burma	36.1	180	58
India	749.2	260	56
China	1,029.2	310	69
Pakistan	92.4	380	51
Vietnam	60.1	n.a.	n.a.
36 countries	2,390	260	60

Middle Income Economies

Indonesia	158.9	540	55
Philippines	53.4	660	63
Egypt	45.9	720	60
Nigeria	96.5	730	50
Thailand	50.0	860	64
Turkey	48.4	1,160	64
Brazil	132.6	1,720	64
Mexico	76.8	2,040	66
South Korea	40.1	2,110	68
South Africa	31.6	2,340	54
Iran	43.8	n.a.	61
60 countries	1,188	1,250	61

	Population (millions) 1984	Per capita GNP (dollars)	Life expectancy at birth (years) 1984
High Income Oil Exporters			
Saudi Arabia	11.1	10,530	62
Total	18.6	11,250	62
Industrial Market Economies			
Spain	38.7	4,440	77
Italy	57.0	6,420	77
Great Britain	56.4	8,570	74
France	54.9	9,760	77
Japan	120.0	10,630	77
West Germany	61.2	11,130	75
United States	237.0	15,390	76
19 countries	733.4	11,430	76
East European Nonmarket Economies			
Poland	36.9	2,100	71
USSR	275.0	n.a.	67

n.a.: not available

The United States and Canada are included with the 19 industrial market economies which have an average per capita
GNP of $11,430. Finally, the eight East European nonmarket
economies (often referred to as the Warsaw Pact countries) are
listed but no figures are given for per capita GNP. It is
unusually difficult to make accurate comparisons of their GNP
with those of market-oriented economies because they calcu-
late GNP by different rules. It is likely that most of them would
fall in the same income level as the upper-middle-income

group noted above with average incomes of about $2000. It
should be noted that the People's Republic of China, though
having an economic system which resembles that of the
Warsaw Pact countries, is included with the group of low income countries by the World Bank tables. Its per capita GNP
was reported to be $310 in 1984.

The Weakness of GNP Statistics
So we now know which are some of the poor countries and
which are some of the rich countries. We know the approxi-
mate level of their per capita incomes. These figures are helpful
in identifying the rich and poor countries, but we should be
careful not to treat the figures with mathematical exactness.
What are some of the pitfalls?

In the first place, many of the poorer countries' figures dis-
play what one economist has called "statistical nakedness." By
this he meant that the staff of government statisticians collecting the information was too small for the complexity of the
task. Another economist found a staff of only two persons
collecting national income figures for a country of 50 million
people.

In the second place, much of the consumption and investment in poor countries is not made in monetary terms at all.
This is true both of highly developed economies and of LDCs,
but nonmonetary consumption and investment represents a
much larger share of the GNP of LDCs. If the U.S. national income statisticians, in their calculation of the total U.S. GNP,
overlook the lettuce I grow in my backyard garden, it won't
make much of a difference. But poor countries are largely
"subsistence" economies. From 80 to 90 percent of all of their
consumption is not bought with money, but is produced on
their own small farms and shops. They are producing these
items for home consumption rather than for sale on the market.

The same thing is true of their investment expenditures.
Even the school buildings are often built with volunteer labor.
Few materials need to be purchased and little hired labor is
used. In the cattle-raising economies of Africa, much of the investment consists of enlarging the size of their herds. The size

of this kind of investment can be estimated only very roughly, if it is included in the GNP statistics at all.

So if we define GNP as the total of consumer expenditure, investment expenditure, and government expenditure, it is very clear that two of these three elements in LDCs are very inaccurate guesses at best. The government expenditure figures are, of course, much more accurate than the other two.

For most poor countries, government expenditures are growing. And because they are growing, their statisticians may feel that their GNP is increasing satisfactorily. But increases in government expenditures may be for modern military equipment which the big powers are eager to sell to them, or for show places such as Africa Hall in Ethiopia or for the modern airport facilities they want for promoting tourism. They may also represent expenditures for ill-conceived power projects such as the huge Volta Dam in Ghana. Expenditures of this kind do not increase the real welfare of their people. Furthermore, some experts who have studied these figures believe that there is a natural bias toward exaggerating GNP growth. The government statisticians know that their top government officials would like to see "growth."

But there are still other problems. After GNP figures are collected, they are expressed in the national currency of that country. To compare them with those of the United States, they must be converted to U.S. dollars. This is a simple task when applied to developed countries. Most developed countries have relatively free markets for foreign exchange. If I wish to travel in England, for instance, I can go to my bank in even such a small city as Goshen, Indiana, and buy British pounds. Or I may, if I prefer, wait to do so until I arrive in England. In either case the figure which is used to convert one currency into equivalent value in another currency is the exchange rate.

But there is no free market for the foreign exchange of many countries—particularly not for that of the poor countries. Official exchange rates often reflect the tendency to overvalue the currency of the poorer countries. And in any event, the exchange rates have significance only for internationally traded goods. They obviously do not apply to goods or services which cannot enter into international exchange.

When I was in New Delhi in India I needed a haircut. I was able to get one in a hotel barbershop for 10 rupees—about $1 U.S. This is only about a tenth of what one would pay for a haircut in a big city hotel in the U.S., but it was still more than I would have paid if I had employed one of the barbers who set up shop on the streets. The rupee-dollar exchange rate was 10 to 1 but this exchange rate obviously did not apply to service items like haircuts.

In a rural village north of Calcutta there are two Christian churches, a Methodist and an Anglican. I heard that the salary of the Methodist pastor was only 100 rupees a month. At the official exchange rate this would be only $10 U.S. My taxi bill round trip from Calcutta to the village was 130 rupees. The pastor was certainly better off than an American with a $10 monthly income. But he was still very, very poor. The official church discipline did not permit the pastor to supplement his income by outside employment. The official exchange rate may make his poverty appear to be worse than it actually is. But at *any* conceivable exchange rate he was certainly one of the world's poor.

Other Ways to Measure Economic Well-Being

Differences in GNP from one country to another are very large and the gross differences certainly have some significance. But they form only one way of differentiating between the poor and the rich nations. The World Bank publishes many other kinds of statistics which relate to the "physical quality of life index" (PQLI). PQLI combines such things as life expectancy, infant mortality, and literacy. The first two of these show the effects of nutrition, public health, and the general environment, as well as income. Literacy reflects general well-being, and as I shall show in chapter 5, it also is a requirement for economic development.

The average life expectancy at birth in 1984 was only 60 years in the low-income economies whereas it was 76 years in the industrial market economies like the U.S. Infant mortality rates were 72 per 1000 in the poor countries compared with 9 per 1000 in the rich. Average daily calorie supply per capita in 1983 was 2,336 in the poor countries, 3,352 in the rich. Of the people of high school age in 1983, 31 percent were enrolled in school in the poor countries, 85 percent in the rich.

The United Nations Institute for Social Studies in Geneva has been working on the development of some physical indicators of real consumption levels. In addition to calorie intake and school enrollment, they are trying to include such things as housing space, shoe and cloth consumption, radios, bicycles, and other consumer durables per capita.

I once heard the late Dudley Seers, British expert on economic development, speak at an economics club meeting in Addis Ababa, Ethiopia. In a whimsical remark he said, "Whenever I go to a new country, I first look at people's feet. Are they barefoot? Are they wearing sandals? or cheap shoes of local make? or more substantial imported shoes?" He expressed the opinion that this "shoe standard" would correlate rather well with real consumption levels. I should add that he made this statement before it was popular in the mid-1960s for Western college students to go barefoot!

The *World Development Report 1981* gives the results of an attempt to make a comparison between the purchasing power of people in the poor and rich countries based on real income rather than money income which has been converted into dollars at prevailing exchange rates. The latter measure shows the industrial countries have 48 times the average purchasing power of the poor countries. But in terms of real income the disparity is only 12 times. This still is unfortunately high, but it is not as unconscionable as money income comparisons would imply.

Sri Lanka is an example of a country which has achieved a much better quality of life than its relatively low money income would suggest. It had a per capita GNP of only $360 in 1984, thus placing it in the low-income economy category. But its life expectancy at birth was 70 years—a figure which was above the average of the upper-middle-income countries and only six years less than the United States. Its infant mortality rate and its literacy rate were also well above the average of upper-middle-income countries. This is a remarkable achievement. It shows that a country with a low income can realize a physical quality of life which is superior to that of countries enjoying six times Sri Lanka's income level.

Finally, per capita GNP can at best be only an indicator of economic well-being. It says nothing about a country's cultural values. Many LDCs have a rich, culturally diverse heritage. The people in these countries enjoy satisfactions which ultimately are of greater importance than the cold economic indicators would imply.

In this chapter I have sought to answer the question of how poor the people in the LDCs are. But I haven't said anything about how many people live in these poor countries. The population of some of them is very small. In fact, *World Development Report 1986* lists 34 "countries" with populations of less than a million persons each. For example, Grenada, which American marines "rescued from communism," has a population of less than 100,000. Most of these small countries should also be classified as LDCs, the only exceptions are Iceland, Luxembourg, the Bahamas, Bahrain, and Qatar.

India, with a population of 749 million, is sometimes called the largest LDC, but this ignores China with a population of over a billion people. The World Bank estimates that in 1984 the total population of all LDCs was 3.6 billion. This compares with only 733 million for the industrial market economies and 389 million for the Warsaw Pact countries of Eastern Europe. Although, as I shall point out in chapter 2, a few people in the LDCs are rich (a tiny elite, very rich), the vast majority of the nearly 4 billion people in LDCs are poor.

Per capita GNP statistics say nothing about the distribution of income. The general welfare of a country as a whole with a relatively equal distribution of wealth and income is much superior to that of another country with the same per capita GNP but marked inequality in its distribution.

What is poverty? As one tours through the back country of many of the LDCs, one observes that the people are eating. They are not eating very well by American standards, but they are probably better fed than their parents or grandparents were. They have simple houses, often with only straw or palm leaves for roofs, but at least they keep out the rain. In the warm climates where many of the poor live, heating is no problem, though large numbers no doubt suffer during the chilly nights. They have clothing which covers the body and which is adequate by local custom.

In what sense are these people worse off than the rural Spanish or Irish? They are subject to disease which reduces their energy level and shortens their lives. Furthermore, nearly half of them are illiterate. This often produces a limited ability to comprehend simple ideas and to make elementary calculations. Thus it is difficult for them to participate in economic change. The stark fact is not that they derive less consumer satisfaction than the rural Frenchman or Italian; it is, rather, that they are poor as human beings. It is to a better understanding of this poverty that this book is directed.

Questions for further study and discussion

1. What elements would you use to define the poverty or wealth of a country?

2. What are the weaknesses in the concept of GNP as a measure of the welfare of a nation's people? Can you think of weaknesses other than those which were outlined in this chapter?

3. The eastern European countries (Warsaw Pact nations) have lower per capita GNPs than the Western European nations, the United States, Canada, and Japan. Can you think of reasons other than the efficiency or inefficiency of the economic system which may account for part of these differences?

4. If you were constructing a physical quality of life index, what elements would you include?

2

What Are Poor Countries Like?

It is difficult to define the characteristics of poor countries because they are so heterogeneous. I have already noted in chapter 1 that they are not equally poor. In this chapter I will make generalizations about poor countries, but in all cases there are exceptions to the features I will list. With nearly 100 countries included in the category of LDCs, it would be strange, indeed, if there were not many differences between them. Yet, the similarities are sufficiently strong that they can still usefully be described as a group.

Because of differences between LDCs, some have tried to find subtypes. In chapter 1 I mentioned the World Bank groupings which were made by income level: low income, lower middle income, and upper middle income. Others have defined types by geographical areas. Thus they speak of an African type which contains most of the poorest of the LDCs and tends to have a substantial amount of land relative to population. However, much of the land is desert or tropical rain forest not suitable for cultivation. The Asian type generally has a greater population density and usually this fact itself contributes to the low levels of income which obtain. Generally the Latin-American type has a higher income level and probably a greater potential for further development.

A Colonial Past

Many of today's LDCs had a long past history as colonies of a major political power. This is especially true of the LDCs in Africa. At the end of World War II there were only two independent countries in all of Africa, and even in 1957 there were only four: Egypt, Ethiopia, Liberia, and the Union (now Republic) of South Africa. In 1957 the former British colony Gold Coast became the nation of Ghana, and in the years since then, 33 other nations in Africa became independent.

The geographical boundaries of these countries were often determined by the power politics of European states. Little attention was paid to economic considerations or to ethnic or tribal loyalties. Thus, Nigeria, the most populous of the new African countries, included four major tribal groups: Yoruba, Ibo, Hausa, and Fulani—along with a number of smaller ethnic groups. Conflicts between the Ibo and the other groups caused the Ibo nation (Biafra) to secede and resulted in a bloody civil war.

More than 40 languages are spoken by members of 110 different ethnic groups in the Sudan. Across this huge country (more than four times the size of France), much of which is desert and swamp, there is only one paved inter-city road. How can such an area develop the sense of national unity that we usually associate with a modern nation-state?

One story of the arbitrary (even whimsical) way in which the colonial powers drew boundaries relates to the boundary between Tanzania and Kenya. When this boundary was originally drawn, Tanzania was called Tanganyika and it was to be a German colony. (At the end of World War I Tanganyika became a British mandate under the League of Nations.) The Kaiserin of Germany is said to have complained that she had no major mountains within her possessions. So to please her, the boundary line was drawn with a hump so that Mount Kilimanjaro would be in Tanganyika rather than in Kenya!

As satellites of major powers, these colonies were expected to serve the "mother country" as sources of raw materials and as markets for manufactured goods. In the pursuit of this goal, Great Britain imposed restrictive tariffs and quotas on textile imports from colonial India. This crippled India's cloth production in the interest of Leeds and Halifax.

When the mother country built roads (and sometimes railroads) in the colonies, they were built to fulfill the economic objective of the colonial power. Thus the late Barbara Ward, well-known British student of LDCs, observed that transportation maps of Africa make it appear that the colonial powers were trying to drain Africa of its resources. They show the main arteries of traffic going from the interior to the seacoast. The transportation facilities were obviously not designed to facilitate trade from one part of the colony to another. When the colonies gained their independence and attempted to become nations, they did not have the transportation systems which would have contributed to nationhood. These and other economic patterns of the past were continued after independence. So the new nations often felt that their former political colonial status had been replaced by a new form of colonialism—economic.

I do not mean to imply that a colonial past inevitably must result in barriers to economic development. It is appropriate for citizens of present-day Canada and the United States to remember that they, too, had a colonial past. Like the ex-colonies I have described in the paragraphs above, Canada and the United States were milked for their raw materials. Their transportation system was built originally for exports. The boundary between Canada and the United States was drawn arbitrarily. Even after independence, these countries are still large exporters of raw materials, and they continue to work assiduously to improve their ability to export raw materials. It is even rumored that officials in countries like Ethiopia and Liberia complain that some of their problems stem from a lack of foreign investment which they would have enjoyed if they had a colonial past.

Poor Government

Many LDCs are hampered by poor government. The discipline and drive which characterize socialist governments like the People's Republic of China are often lacking. So also are the well-developed political parties which vie for leadership in the industrialized countries. In the great majority of LDCs, the typical pattern is either a one-party civilian rule or a military dictatorship. Some countries have fluctuated between these two patterns over the years. Sometimes elections are held and the military recedes into the background. But when the civilian rulers can't maintain law and order, there will be a military coup and a military dictatorship will once again emerge.

Whether the LDC is ruled by a one-party civilian government or by a military dictatorship, the ruling group tends to be a relatively small oligarchy. This elite, which lives in the capital city, usually has only a thin base of popular support. As a result the ordinary citizen, and particularly the peasant farmer, will likely view the government with apprehension and suspicion. For example, peasants who are members of the Masai tribe in Kenya are likely to think of themselves as being Masai rather than Kenyan. To many natives of Bali, Java is a distant country rather than another part of their own nation of Indonesia.

Where there is only a one-party civilian government or a military dictatorship, there is really no provision for an orderly transfer of power; the government is inevitably unstable. One government is succeeded by another as a result of a coup rather than an election.

In 1963, at the time of the assassination of President John F. Kennedy, I was living in Ethiopia. There were a number of Kenyan students in the university where I was teaching. Kennedy was a popular president and these students extended to me their profound condolences. In fact the university was closed for several days in Kennedy's honor. But as I talked with the students, I could tell that they were concerned not only about the death of Kennedy but about the future of the United States. They had much difficulty understanding how the government could shift quickly and peacefully from the Kennedy to the Johnson administration. An orderly transfer of power was not within the range of their experience.

In the early history of some of the newly independent African countries, political parties were organized. It appeared to some that they might develop multiparty governments typical of the colonial powers who formerly controlled them. However, membership in the parties tended to be determined by ethnic background rather than by ideological differences.

In some newly independent LDCs, minority ethnic groups have been absorbed peacefully. This is especially true where the country has been led by a strong and charismatic person. In other cases bitter fighting has resulted—in some cases even approaching the genocide of minority groups. Under such circumstances, the first concern of the government is to remain in power. This obviously does not contribute to long-range planning. The leadership is more preoccupied with objectives of security and prestige. Low salaries for government workers may encourage them to supplement their salaries by accepting bribes. Or it may encourage the more able workers to seek employment in agencies of the United Nations or to join the "brain drain" to the developed countries.

The suppression of ethnic minorities has at times resulted both in much suffering and in the stifling of economic growth. In Southeast Asia, Chinese who left their native country (in some cases two or three generations ago) have become leaders in business and the professions. They have thus enjoyed standards of living above that of the indigenous peoples. This has sometimes led to jealousy of, discrimination against, and even the suppression of, the overseas Chinese.

Similarly, people from India often became the entrepreneurs in East African countries. It is said that President Amin expelled 45,000 Asians from Uganda in 1972. Many of these Asians came from India at a time when India was a part of the British Empire and settled in Uganda when it, too, was a part of the British Empire. The expulsion or suppression of these capable Indians will inevitably militate against the economic development of Uganda.

Subsistence Production and Self-Employment

Another pervasive characteristic of most LDCs is that most people are self-employed. They spend most of their time producing food for their own home consumption. They also build their simple houses and the scant furniture which they contain.

Clothing, too, is largely homemade. In his study of Nigeria and Pakistan, Wayne Nafziger reported that "the overwhelming majority of the population" were " 'self employed' in agriculture, petty trade, or crafts. Thus, in Nigeria wage-paid employment comprised only about 5 percent of the economically active population." In Pakistan the figure was 8 percent.

Economic development will mean a gradual shift from subsistence production to wage employment. This will be accompanied by a gradual increase of production of goods for sale on the market relative to those produced for home consumption. The market may be a foreign one, in which case the money gained from exports may be used to buy imported products which, hopefully, will improve the standard of living. The appearance of these foreign goods will serve to stimulate the national population to work harder and to spend more time producing the export crop. One economist who studied the rapid rise of Nigerian cocoa production after 1900 found that it did not result in a decrease in the output of subsistence food production. Rather, it resulted in the use of previously underemployed workers and of previously uncultivated land.

The dominance of subsistence production may also be changed when foreign mining or plantation enterprises come to the area. Some firms bring in their own labor and imported foodstuffs and thus have only a minimal interaction with the indigenous self-sufficient economy. But most hire local labor and purchase at least some local foodstuffs. This leads to a rise of food marketing, and the wage payments contribute to the same result.

I do not mean to suggest that self-employment will eventually disappear as a country develops. Self-employment is not necessarily associated with poverty. Indeed, it is also the dream and happily the realization of many successful American entrepreneurs.

Rapid Population Growth

The World Bank reports that the average annual growth of population for the LDCs of the low-income category during the past 10 years was 2.0 percent. But for the LDCs in the lower-middle-income group, it was 2.4 percent. During the decade of the 1960s the growth was even greater—2.3 percent annually for the low-income countries and 2.6 percent for the lower-middle-income group.

In spite of the poverty of the less developed countries, their populations were growing more than twice as fast as those of the rich industrial market economies. The rate of growth for the rich countries for 1965-73 was 1.1 percent and for 1973-83 was 0.7 percent. One can even ask whether the high rates of population growth in the LDCs were not in themselves a cause of the poverty.

The LDCs have faster rates of population growth than the presently rich countries experienced when their economies started to develop rapidly in the "takeoff" of the eighteenth and nineteenth centuries. As the Industrial Revolution came to the older industrial economies, these countries had birth rates of approximately 35 per 1,000. But the death rates were also nearly as high and so the population increase was slow. During the nineteenth century, the death rate fell gradually but steadily. This was partly a result of the growing number of doctors, nurses, and hospitals and of an improvement in the quality of their services. There were better water supplies for the cities and modern sewage systems were being built. Systematic garbage and refuse disposal was organized. These improvements together with medical research resulted in better techniques for controlling epidemic diseases. In the twentieth century the development of antibiotics also contributed tremendously to the control of infectious diseases.

As the death rates went down there was little immediate effect on the birth rates. This meant that there was a large "population bulge." In 1800 this frightened the English parson-economist Thomas R. Malthus who predicted that population would soon outstrip the means of supporting the population and that "misery" would result. But Malthus was wrong in his forecasts for nineteenth century England. Eventually the birth rate fell, the rate of population growth declined, and the productivity of the economy increased enormously.

The reasons for the declining birth rate are well-known. More people were living in cities, and urban families tended to be smaller than rural. There was an increased knowledge of contraceptive techniques. With the higher-income levels becoming more pervasive, the pattern of life changed. Social convention had shifted from the large to the small family. The "once for all" population spurt was followed by a new pattern in which birth rates fell to 15 to 20 per 1000 and the death rates to approximately 10 per 1000. Population growth in the rich countries as a whole is now less than one percent per year. Some countries already are facing an actual decline in population. The World Bank studies indicate that sometime between 2000 and 2010 A.D.—in both the industrial countries as a group and for the Eastern European nonmarket economies—population will stabilize.

The pattern of population growth for the LDCs is different. They had the latecomer's advantage of being able to borrow advanced medical technology from the developed countries. As a result, their death rates have fallen much more rapidly than they did in the rich countries.

LDCs have reduced their death rates in a period of from 10 to 20 years as much as the rich countries did in a period of 50 to 100 years. As a result their population bulge has occurred much more suddenly. In some LDCs birth rates have remained near their biological maximum. They have shown only a small tendency to decline.

The rapid growth of population in LDCs has not always posed an immediate problem. Some countries of Africa and Latin America (as well as certain areas in Asia) still have cultivable land which is not being fully used. But even in such countries, most if not all of this land will certainly be placed under cultivation within 20 or 30 years.

But it is in countries which are already densely settled that the rapidly expanding population poses the most serious threat. One such country, China, has been attempting to enforce a one-child family policy to cope with this threat. Methods of reducing the rate of population growth will be analyzed in more detail in chapter 3.

Growth of Cities

The rapid increase in population has been accompanied by migration to the cities. Only 22.2 percent of the population of LDCs lived in cities in 1950. By 1980 this percentage had grown to 35.4 and by the year 2000 it is estimated that it will reach 43.3. Indeed, the United Nations estimates that by the year 2000 20 of the 25 world's largest cities (cities with population of over 10 million) will be located in the LDCs. These 20 cities will include such enormous urban agglomerations as Mexico City, with a population forecast of 31 million people; São Paulo (Brazil), with nearly 26 million; and Shanghai (China), with nearly 23 million.

What will be the plight of these urban peoples? Although they migrated to the cities to improve their standards of living, the cities have rarely provided enough jobs to make this possible. More and more people try to engage in retail trade or to give services which require little capital. This is apparent to anyone who has visited an LDC. Whenever I would leave our home in Addis Ababa, Ethiopia, I would be accosted by three or four shoeshine boys who wanted to polish my shoes for the equivalent of about 4 cents of U.S. money. It was a dusty country and I usually needed the shoeshine, but I could give the job to only one of the four boys. After he had polished my shoes he became effectively unemployed (as were the others who were with him), until some one else came along. I did not see the homes where these boys lived, but I know that near all large cities in LDCs there are "shantytowns" where the roofs and walls are not adequate to keep out the rain and where sanitary facilities are either completely lacking or totally inadequate. Urban life in an LDC may be grim indeed.

Unemployment and Disguised Unemployment

Some of the people who make up the rapidly growing population of the cities were born there, but most probably migrated from the rural areas. Having six to ten times as many people trying to polish shoes as are needed is really a form of "disguised unemployment." However, many of the people who migrated to the cities from the rural areas were also not fully employed in the farming communities from which they came.

One economist has reported that his study revealed that three people from the rural areas came to look for each new job which was opened in the cities. In other words, the greatest of all economic resources—labor resources—are not being fully used in LDCs. This, indeed, is one of the major reasons they are poor.

Many other examples could be given of poorly employed human resources. There is heavy pressure on government departments to employ more clerks and errand persons than are really needed. Similarly, people are urged to hire more domestic servants than can effectively be used.

Like most Americans, our family doesn't regularly employ any domestic servants. But when we were living in Ethiopia we had a full-time servant. Although our apartment was small we had few of the labor-saving devices to which we were accustomed in the U.S. Our drinking water had to be both filtered and boiled, our clothes had to be hand-washed in the bathtub, shopping trips required much time, and we couldn't buy prepared foods. For example, when we wanted to eat chicken, our servant went to a local market to buy the birds live. He then tied them to the front door of our apartment until he took them to the backyard to slaughter them and prepare them for our table. He was with us only a short time until he made it clear that he was overworked. We had to employ a cleaning lady half-time to assist him. Other expatriate friends often had many more servants than we had.

After returning from Ethiopia, I was asked to give several talks on economic development at a college in an Eastern city. In the audience was a Tanzanian national who had a short-term teaching appointment at the college. After my talk he came to me and said: "I hope that my country never becomes so highly developed that my wife has to do her own housework." He had lived in the U.S. long enough that, although he didn't know me personally, he was sure that my wife had no servants to help with the housework. I didn't take the time to explain to him that the main reason his wife did not have to do her own housework was that the rates of pay for domestic servants were so low in his country that living standards for domestics were vastly below his own. In contrast, if we want to employ domestic servants in our homes in a developed country, we must pay them at rates which will enable them to have a standard of living not far below that of our own.

Inequality in Wealth and Income

This leads me to discuss another characteristic feature of the poor countries. Not only is their average standard of living lower than that of the rich countries; there is greater inequality between the rich and the poor. In chapter 1, I recounted the weaknesses of using GNP as a measure of relative income. If we don't know precisely what GNP is, how can we know whether it is more unequally distributed in poor countries than in rich? Of course we can't know for sure, but a casual observation will reveal that even in some of the poorest countries there are some people who are very rich. They have large homes, many servants, fine motor cars, Swiss bank accounts, and they spend much of their time abroad living in luxury.

The World Bank has published data which have been gathered by a joint project of the World Bank and the International Labour Organisation. They do not have data for all countries, so they do not attempt to prepare averages. But the data presented for individual countries are interesting.

They show the share of household incomes received by the five "quintiles" of the population and also by the top 10 percent. If income were equally distributed among these various groups, each quintile would have 20 percent of the total income and the top 10 percent of the population would, of course, have 10 percent of the income.

No country, rich or poor, comes close to this ideal equal distribution of income. Perhaps the socialist countries of Eastern Europe come the closest to it, but the World Bank does not provide figures for these countries and so we can only surmise. But it does give figures for the rich industrial nations. For the United States in 1980 the poorest 20 percent of the households received only 5.3 percent of the income, whereas the wealthiest 20 percent received 39.9 percent. Some of the other rich industrial nations had a distribution of income more equal than the United States. For example, in the Netherlands, the poorest 20 percent received 8.3 percent of the income and the richest 20 percent received 36.2 percent.

Compare these figures with some of the LDCs. In Kenya, for example, the poorest 20 percent received only 2.6 percent of the income while the richest 20 percent received 60.4 percent. In Peru the corresponding figures were 1.9 and 61.0; in Brazil they were 2.0 and 66.6.

The poverty of the poor in these poor countries is so pervasive that it is not helpful to say that GNP is growing. We must know whether it is growing so that all classes of the population are growing richer or whether most, if not all, of the newly gained riches are simply adding to the affluence of the already wealthy elite of these countries. It may only mean that the balances in their Swiss bank accounts are growing.

Nature of LDC Foreign Trade and Dependence on Exports

International trade is an important part of the economic life of all countries. Usually it is of more importance in small countries than in large. Large countries have trade within their borders which would have been trade between countries if they were divided into smaller units. In the United States, for example, if the 13 original colonies had become separate countries instead of parts of a large nation, much of the domestic trade which now goes on within the United States would have been international trade. LDCs may be large (e.g., India), but many of them are small. The volume of foreign trade in a large country tends to be small relative to their GNP. Conversely, the ratio of trade to GNP is large in small countries such as Jamaica.

Even where the developed countries are relatively small (e.g., Belgium or the Netherlands), they tend to trade mainly with other developed countries. LDCs on the other hand, tend to have most of their foreign trade not with other LDCs, but with the developed nations. This is partly a result of their colonial heritage. When they were colonies of a great power, they naturally traded with that power, sending them raw materials and receiving manufactured goods in return. The continuation of this type of trade after independence results in what I referred to in an earlier paragraph as "economic colonialism."

LDCs do not trade with each other in part because of the fact that many of these countries are close together geographically and tend to produce the same products. Thus they compete with each other. The "banana republics" of Central America would have little occasion to sell their bananas to other banana-producing countries of their region. In 1984 only 15 percent of the exports of Honduras went to other LDCs, but 81 percent of their exports went to developed countries. In contrast, 90 percent of all exports from Norway went to other developed countries.

Still another reason for the small amount of trade between one LDC and another is that the transportation facilities were not built with this in mind. Many LDCs which are located side-by-side are not connected with a single railroad. Railroads, if they exist at all, were built to take products from the interior to the seacoast. From there they can be shipped almost as easily to a developed country on some other continent as to an LDC near by.

Exports form a large part of the GNP of many of the smaller LDCs. For example, in 1984, 34 percent of the GNP of Costa Rica consisted of exports of goods and services. Malaysia had an even higher proportion, 56 percent; and Jamaica, 55 percent.

Not only are exports vital to the economy of the smaller LDCs; their exports often consist largely of only one or two primary products. For example, exports of coffee from Ethiopia are larger than all other exports combined. For other LDCs, the major export may be sugar, cocoa, tea, tin, rubber, bauxite, or oil. We use the term "mono-culture" to characterize such economies. If the one major export is oil, for example, the exporting country will have prospered in the 1970s but will have been adversely affected by the decline in the price of crude oil in the mid-1980s.

An LDC which is largely dependent upon the export of a single primary raw material is at the mercy of many forces beyond its control. It is dependent upon export earnings. But these earnings tend to fluctuate—often wildly. If the product is an agricultural product, the export volume will fluctuate because of variations in the yield of the crop caused by the vagaries of the weather. The size of the foreign demand depends on the prosperity of the importing countries. World prices fluctuate because of both these variations in demand and because of the variation in supplies of other producing countries.

Economists would say that LDCs which export only a few primary products often suffer from the adverse effects of a low "price elasticity" of demand. This simply means that a change in the price of the product sold will result in a relatively smaller change in the quantity sold. When the price of the product falls on the world market, incomes fall sharply. Recent examples of this include such products as cocoa, sisal, and copper.

We are well aware of the changes in the price of crude oil. An export cartel (OPEC) has tried to stabilize it at a high level. The price of oil increased sharply in the 1970s. In the 1980s the price fell. But the price of some other products has shown an even greater fluctuation. For example, the world price of sugar was 14 cents a pound in January 1974. It rose to 58 cents in December 1974, was down to 18 cents in July 1975, and in 1985 was only 3.5 cents. One can imagine what kind of havoc these fluctuations caused for countries whose primary export was sugar.

Two other factors have tended to hold down the price of some primary raw materials. One is what economists call a low "income elasticity of demand" in the developed countries. This simply means that as incomes rise, people do not increase their purchases of some products as much as their incomes increase. In fact, higher incomes may even result in smaller purchases of some products, such as potatoes.

The other factor is that synthetic substitutes have been developed for some primary products. Synthetic rubber has reduced the demand for natural rubber. Rayon has reduced the demand for cotton and silk.

The combination of these factors has adversely affected the "terms of trade" of many countries. This is a technical term which refers to the ratio of a country's export prices to its import prices. If prices of the products they export fall while the prices of the items they import rise, we say that the terms of trade have worsened. Deterioration in the terms of trade may also result when both export and import prices are rising, but the prices of the imported products are rising at a more rapid rate.

A simple way of thinking of terms of trade is to ask, "How many bushels of wheat do you need to sell to buy a tractor?" American farmers have been very conscious of this problem as tractor prices have increased and wheat prices have stabilized or fallen. (Of course a 1986 tractor is more expensive than a 1946 tractor partly because it is a superior machine.)

The World Bank reported that the terms of trade for many LDCs have fallen since 1980. Fourteen of the 28 low-income countries reporting show a worsening in their terms of trade. Only 15 of the 50 middle-income countries show an improvement in the terms of trade, and these are largely the oil producing countries such as Indonesia, Mexico, and Iraq. The other side of this picture is that 48 of the 79 poorer countries have suffered from a deterioration in their terms of trade. This means that it is harder for them to import the items they need for their development. It is also difficult for them to pay the interest and retire the principal on their debts.

Small Public Sectors

A large part of the economies of socialist countries consist of their public sectors. Usually all manufacturing, except that done by the small craftsman, is done by industries which are governmentally owned. Transportation and communication facilities, the construction industry and even a large share of the retail establishments are owned and operated by the government. In other words, the public sector is the great bulk of a socialist economy.

However, in many of the wealthy capitalist industrial countries, the public sector has been growing. The largest automobile factory in France is governmentally owned as are most of the commercial banks. Coal mining has been nationalized in England. In much of Europe transportation and communication facilities are governmentally owned. Even in the United States our largest universities and most of our elementary and secondary schools are governmentally owned. The same is true of our highways and many of our hospitals.

Many LDCs claim to have socialist governments. But for the most part their economies are not, in fact, socialist. In part this arises because of the preponderance of subsistence production and self-employment already noted. Public consumption represented only 13 percent of the GNP of low-income and middle-income countries in 1984. In contrast it represented 17 percent on the average in industrial countries. It was considerably higher in countries like Sweden and Denmark, where the percentages were 28 and 26 respectively.

Conclusion

In this chapter I have described the main characteristics of LDCs. It is easier to do this than to suggest changes which will enable these countries substantially to improve their living standards. But it is to this task to which my attention must now turn.

Questions for further study and discussion

1. Many of the world's poor countries were at one time colonies of countries which are now rich. To what extent was their colonial past a cause of the poverty of these poor countries? Did they benefit in any way from their former colonial status?

2. Do you feel that countries having two or more political parties and free elections are more likely to develop satisfactorily than countries ruled by a military dictatorship or an undemocratic single-party civilian government? Why? What are some of the advantages of each?

3. What are the advantages and disadvantages of subsistence employment compared with working for wages?

4. For people who live in LDCs, what are the relative advantages of city life and rural life?

5. Why are the populations of LDCs growing more rapidly today than did the populations of Western Europe, the United

States, and Canada at any time in their history?

6. Should a country seeking to develop sacrifice the goal of greater equality in the distribution of wealth and income to the goal of increasing the total size of its wealth and income? Why or why not?

7. Should an LDC seek to improve its economic position by expanding its exports or by concentrating its attention on producing more of the products it needs for its own consumption?

3

Reducing the Rate of Population Growth

In chapter 2, I indicated that rapid population growth was one of the characteristics of LDCs. I pointed out that population was growing much more rapidly in LDCs than in the richer countries and that much of this growth is occurring in the cities. Every year the world's population increases by 82 million persons. At this rate, in three years the world's population will grow by the equivalent of the present population of the United States. But most of these additional people will be born in the poor countries. If present trends continue, most of the world's largest cities in the year 2000 will be in the poor countries.

Does the world have adequate resources to feed additional millions of people? Will the use of the world's resources simply to maintain life mean that these resources will not be available to provide the means of economic growth and so lift the poor countries out of their poverty?

As I will note below, there is no universal agreement on the seriousness of the population problem. It is clear that the economic welfare of any nation is simply the total economic product of that nation divided by the number of people who must share it. If we think of the economic product as being a fixed quantity, it is obvious that the more people make use of it, the smaller will be the quantity going to each person.

But the economic product is not fixed. The more people there are, the more goods and services will be produced. Will the additional production be increased in proportion to the growth of the population? more than in proportion? or less than in proportion? Because the resources of the world are not infinite, it is widely thought that for many countries the additional production will be less than the increase of the population. Where this is the case a reduction in the rate of population growth is one of the most urgent problems to be addressed if the welfare of the poor nations is to be enhanced.

The staff of the World Bank believes that this is such an important problem that they have made it the main focus of the *World Development Report 1984*. I have drawn heavily on this report in writing this chapter. I would urge readers who would like to study the problem in greater depth to read the entire report. Many tables and charts are also provided in the report to elaborate on the points made.

I will consider four major questions as I outline the population problem:

(1) Why is the population in the LDCs increasing more rapidly than in the rich countries?

(2) What are the problems which rapid population growth creates for the poor countries?

(3) What measures can be taken which will reduce the rate of population growth?

(4) Is there a specifically Christian perspective which should be considered in analyzing the population problem?

Why do LDCs have such high rates of population growth?

In chapter 2, I reported that population increases rapidly because birth rates remain high while death rates are reduced. What explains the high birth rates? There are at least six reasons.

First, children are considered to be an economic asset in the families of the poor nations. On the other hand, in the rich nations children are considered to be a cost. Newspaper reports in the United States estimate the cost of rearing a child from birth until the child's education is completed at $100,000 or more. During the early years of a child's life the parents may lose time from work to care for the child. Or child care must be provided and this may add to the expense of rearing the child. It may take the time of one or both parents to find proper child care facilities and to take their child to places where this care is provided. To be sure, as the children gets older, they may help with the housework. But one study found that this averaged only an hour a day for children ages 12 to 17 in cities or their suburbs. For children ages six to 11, the household chores performed by children required only a half hour per day.

The contrast between this situation in a typical American urban community and the situation prevailing in LDCs is a sharp one. In Nepalese villages children of only six to eight years of age were found to be spending from three to four hours a day caring for the farm animals and helping their younger brothers and sisters. Teenagers in Java were found to be working from eight to ten hours a day. Those in Bangladesh work even longer hours. In some poor countries children may even contribute cash income to their families. In the Philippines some children in their late teens were found to contribute as much cash income as adults in the same family.

In economics we sometimes think in terms of cost/benefit ratios. In the rich countries, the economic cost of additional children is much greater than the economic benefit they engender. Therefore, families often limit sharply the number of children they have. In the poor countries the costs of additional children are relatively smaller and the benefits they engender relatively greater. Therefore parents in these countries welcome large families.

Second, families in poor countries want a large number of children because many of the children who are born will die in infancy. Thanks to antibiotics and generally improved health care, infant mortality rates have declined in many LDCs, but they are still high. In some parts of Africa one out of five children born dies before reaching the first birthday. In India, Pakistan, and Bangladesh one out of seven infants dies. Parents may feel that they need to have many babies in order to be sure that at least a few survive. But it is the very frequency of births which tends to weaken both the mother and the babies and thus makes them more susceptible to disease.

Third, in poor countries where social security systems are either completely absent or very primitive, parents may regard children as their major source of support during their old age. In one survey of parents in countries as diverse as Thailand, Turkey, Korea, Indonesia, and the Philippines, 80 to 90 percent of the parents said that they expected their children to support them in their old age. These countries are some of the more developed of the LDCs. In still less-developed countries, the percentage would probably be even higher. The parents' need for children to provide "social security" when the parents can no longer work is greater than the immediate costs of having additional children.

Fourth, in the rich countries the education of children is one of the substantial costs which the parents must face. In many of the poor countries, educational opportunities are limited, particularly after the child has reached the age of 12. As a result, children of this age or above are available for full-time work to contribute to the family income. Opportunities for primary education are more likely to be available, but the schools are generally located in the village near enough to the children's home or farm that they can combine work with study. Secondary schooling is out of the question if the student must live away from home or travel long distances to get to school.

Fifth, in some LDCs cultural factors contribute to high birth rates. The Latin-American machismo causes husbands to want more children, even though their wives may be less enthusiastic about it. In some cultures there are relatively few options open to young women. Getting married early and having many children may be regarded as the safest route to a satisfying adulthood.

I recall talking with a missionary who was an elementary school teacher in Ethiopia. I asked her what her greatest educational problems were. She replied "dropouts." This was a time when American educators were especially concerned about high school dropouts. 'Why do they drop out?" I asked. 'The girls often drop out to get married." The thought of these little elementary school girls getting married was a hard one for me to grasp. But the girls (or their parents) must have regarded it as the best available option.

Sixth, birth rates are high in LDCs because contraceptive devices may be unavailable, they may be too expensive for the poorest families, or their use may not be culturally acceptable. Under such circumstances, limiting the number of children may involve sexual abstinence, illegal abortion, or even infanticide. The psychological costs of avoiding pregnancy and limiting family size may be thought to be greater than the costs of having additional children.

How serious are the problems of rapid population growth in LDCs?

Conflicting views

For nearly 200 years there has been deep concern about prospects of overpopulation. I mentioned in chapter 2 the British parson-economist, T. R. Malthus. At the beginning of the nineteenth century he published his famous "First Essay on Population." He took the position that the population would increase by geometric progression while the means of subsistence would increase only by arithmetic progression. Thus, with every generation the population would grow 1, 2, 4, 8, 16, 32, 64, whereas the means of subsistence would grow 1, 2, 3, 4, 5, 6, 7. At this rate by the sixth generation, population would be more than nine times as great as there would be food to feed them. He thought that these would be tendencies that obviously could not, in fact, happen, but that the tendency itself would result in much misery.

Many writers since then have pointed out the error in Malthus' idea. He did not realize that by the end of the nineteenth century the birth rate would fall. He also did not realize the enormous potentialities for increasing the means of subsistence which the Industrial Revolution would bring.

But recently some people have felt that although Malthus' projections for Europe were too pessimistic, they may have a genuine relevance for the poorer nations of the world. It is very likely that the Chinese government's one-child family policy may have stemmed in part from the realization by China's leaders that the unchecked growth of population in China would militate against that country's development. I will say more about China's policy later.

In 1972 the Club of Rome commissioned a group of scholars from the Massachusetts Institute of Technology to ascertain whether population growth and industrial expansion would lead to shortages of natural resources. They published their findings in a book entitled *The Limits to Growth*.[1] They developed a series of models which led them to forecast that standards of living would fall, that the supply of essential resources was limited, and that this, together with high levels of pollution, would lead to a collapse of population within 100 years.

Following the publication of the Club of Rome report, other scholars have pointed to some flaws in their methods of research and consequently in their conclusions. In 1981 Julian Simon, then of the University of Illinois, published a book which took a diametrically opposite position. He entitled his book *The Ultimate Resource*. He said, "The ultimate resource is people—skilled, spirited, and hopeful people who will exert their wills and imaginations for their own benefit, and so, inevitably, for the benefit of us all."[2]

Simon made a number of studies of the prices of essential raw materials and found that they are no higher today in relation to income than they were in the middle of the last century. In spite of the enormous increase in demand caused both by the larger population and our much more highly developed economies, the supply is still adequate. If it were not, prices would have advanced relative to income. But he admits that in the short run (30 to 80 years) even moderate population growth may work against human welfare.

---

1. Donella H. Meadows, et al., *The Limits to Growth*. New York: Universe Books, 1972, 205 pp.

2. Julian L. Simon, *The Ultimate Resource*. Princeton, N.J.: Princeton University Press, 1981, p. 348.

In spite of the degree of difference of opinion concerning the seriousness of the population explosion in the world, there is general agreement that it has already created problems and that more will follow unless the growth is somehow checked. In the paragraphs below I will discuss some of these problems.

Deforestation and Desertification

Anyone who has traveled by air over the continents which contain most of the LDCs (Africa, South America and Asia) cannot help but be impressed that there seem to be large land areas where few people are living. Can these areas be turned into land where food can be produced? The answer in some cases is, yes. But to do so would often have serious side effects.

Less than 200 years ago there was a tropical rain forest which extended around the earth in a large land mass extending approximately 20 degrees north and 20 degrees south of the equator. Today nearly 50 percent of these rain forests have disappeared. They have become instead parcels of farmland interspersed by bare earth and unproductive cattle pastures.

These forests which have become victims of the bulldozer, the ax, and the machete were central to the ecological and the economic life of many LDCs. When the trees are gone there is nothing left to protect the roads in the mountainous and wet areas. Floods and landslides become more frequent and more devastating. As a result, dams silt up and less electricity can be generated. It is estimated that one of the big dams in the Philippines has had its useful life cut from 60 to 32 years because of deforestation.

Firewood is still the major fuel for many LDCs. The World Bank estimates that more than a billion people are now cutting firewood faster than it can be replaced by natural growth. Because population is growing rapidly in such African countries as Tanzania and Gambia, wood is so scarce that each household spends 250 to 300 worker days each year just in gathering the wood it needs for fuel. The price of wood in Ethiopia has increased tenfold during the 1970s. The cost of wood now consumes 20 percent of household income.

The shortage of wood has other serious implications for

everyday life in LDCs. Diseases spread more rapidly when there is not enough fuel to heat food or to boil water. Soybeans are an exceptionally nutritious food. They grow well in countries like Burkina Faso (Upper Volta), but they are not widely used there because they have to be cooked a long time. This would require greater use of increasingly scarce wood.

The expansion of agriculture is another important cause of deforestation. The Food and Agricultural Organization (FAO) has estimated that because of population pressure more than 11 million hectares of forest are cleared each year. But much of this land becomes marginal cropland. It could be saved if it were properly irrigated and fertilized. But the farmers often do not have the resources to do this. As a result the land becomes infertile and eroded. When this happens the farmers clear more forest. Thus the process of deforestation moves forward relentlessly.

The adverse effects of deforestation are not confined to the LDCs. They concern the welfare of people all over the world. Tropical rain forests can absorb and hold vast quantities of fresh water. Little of this water is held in the soil of the forest itself but is recycled into the atmosphere. It then returns to the earth as rain. This recycling process is disturbed where the forests are cut. There is a direct relationship between increased deforestation and reduced levels of rainfall.

Furthermore, green plants use carbon dioxide to make their own food and to supply oxygen as a "waste" product. As rain forests disappear the concentration of carbon dioxide in the atmosphere increases. This can result in a "greenhouse" effect. Ultimately this may lead to warmer climates, to the melting of polar icecaps, and over a long term to increasing the levels of the oceans. Large cities built near the sea may gradually be flooded.

Some of the poorest countries of the world are located at the southern edge of the Sahara Desert—the so-called Sahel. Their problems are aggravated by the fact that the desert is moving southward. *Desertification* is the term we apply to it.

When rains fail to come in adequate amounts, serious droughts result. This has on occasion adversely affected crop production even in the normally highly productive areas of the temperate zones. Even severe droughts, however, seldom last more than a year or so. The land is inherently productive, and when the rains return, it once more yields bountifully. But when land becomes desert, even a return of normal rainfall cannot restore it. Unless costly remedies are taken (and LDCs don't have the resources for this) the land will remain unproductive for generations.

Desertification is not primarily the result of occasional droughts. It is, rather, a direct result of population pressure. More people means more intensive cultivation of land, more overgrazing by domestic animals, and more deforestation. Vegetation is stripped from the topsoil and thus its organic matter and nutrients are lost. This exposes the land to erosion from the sun and wind, and from the rains, too, when they return. Where a large population keeps pressure for production high even during periods of drought, the effort is self-defeating. The natural resilience of the land is lost and permanent degradation has set in.

Desertification has affected not only sub-Saharan Africa but also northwestern Asia and parts of the Middle East. It is estimated that every year nearly 80,000 additional square miles of land become deserts. This is a land area somewhat larger than the state of Washington. The process is accelerating. More than 20 percent of the earth's surface is now directly threatened. This area is populated by 80 million persons who, because of desertification, are threatened with malnutrition and famine or with migration to other areas. Today these areas of plenty are increasingly difficult to find.

Disproportionate Number of Children in the Population
It is estimated that in LDCs about 40 percent of the population is age 15 years or younger. In countries with very rapid population growth, such as Kenya, this proportion is more than 50 percent. This contrasts sharply with the United States or Japan, where only 23 percent of the population is less than 15 years of age. On the other hand, the proportion of old people in the populations of LDCs is smaller than in the rich countries,

even though in the rich countries the elderly constitute only a fraction of the number in the under 15 age-group. The result is that the number of people of working age relative to the young and the old is especially small in LDCs. In Kenya one person of working age must support one who is too young or too old to work. In Japan, on the other hand, two people of working age are available to support one who is either too young or too old to work.

The large number of young people in the LDCs also means that birth rates will remain high in the next generation even if each mother has fewer children. Furthermore, for the next several decades, the number of young people seeking jobs will continue to be high. It is estimated that within the next two decades the working age population of Bangladesh will almost double (from 48 million to 84 million). This, in turn, will contribute to the migration to the cities and attempts to over-cultivate the land.

Faced with this huge number of children, the amount of money which must be invested in education is awesome if literacy is to grow. Kenya faces a doubling or tripling of school-age population by the end of this century. Money spent to educate these children will not be available for other purposes such as better roads, more factories, more power. Will the LDCs sacrifice the capital needed for their development plans to educate their children? Will the quality of the education provided be reduced? Or will a growing number of children be excluded entirely from educational opportunity?

These are the kinds of unpleasant alternatives which must be faced.

What measures can be taken to reduce the rate of population growth?

Some countries have done very little to reduce the rate of population growth. At the other extreme is China, with its policy of one-child families. Various types of in between policies have been followed in other countries. I will make an effort to identify those policies which seem to be most promising.

China's One-Child Policy

China has the largest population of any country of the world. Although estimates differ, it is generally agreed that the population now exceeds one billion people—more than one-fifth of the world's total. In the early days of the communist revolution, China's leaders encouraged large families. By 1971, however, they realized that steps should be taken to reduce sharply the rate of population growth. In that year they announced that the goal would be a population of 1.2 billion by the year 2000.

In 1979 Sichuan province started a program attempting to persuade couples to have no more than one child. Rewards were given to couples who limited their children to one and penalties were imposed on couples who had more than two children. Within a year this became a national policy and all of the provinces were expected to implement it. By 1982 most of them had complied. Thus far the result of this policy seems to be a striking reduction in the number of births. Prior to the program, 21 percent of all births were of first children. Now that ratio is up to nearly 40 percent nationwide. In some of the large cities it is over 80 percent. It is probable that the program is more effective in the urban than in the rural areas.

But the policy has had some very serious side effects. The rate of abortion and probably even of infanticide has increased. Apparently many families are still sufficiently traditional that if they can have only one child they want that child to be a son. As a result, girl babies are neglected even to the point of deliberately allowing them to die. The result is that the number of men in the population relative to women has increased. The 1982 census data showed that there were 108.5 boys for every 100 girls at birth. A study of one-child families in Anhui province indicated that 61 percent of the children of one-child certificate holders were boys.

This also has a profound effect on the traditional old-age security system of China. Governmental old-age security is currently provided chiefly in the cities and only to employees of the government and of government-owned businesses. These employees probably represent not more than 15 percent of the labor force. In rural areas, only one percent of men over 65 and women over 60 actually receive pensions paid from welfare funds. The official policy insists that families must assume the major responsibility for the care of the elderly. But if the one-child family is realized, a couple might have to earn enough to support themselves, their child, and four parents. Will they be able to do this?

The Chinese government has assumed the responsibility for the care of the elderly in the future. But one may question whether it has made a realistic study of the costs of such a policy. When today's young parents have reached their retirement years, there will be far fewer people of working age to support them. The problem is similar to that faced by the social security systems of many of the rich countries. But it is more serious because of the speed with which the change to smaller family size has been made.

Ultimately, the most significant effects of the one-child family may be social. Relationships within the large, traditional family unit have no doubt served to instill respect for authority. This may have helped to create an attitude of submissiveness to the power of the Communist Party and the government. But an only child may be more likely to be doted on by parents and grandparents. This may make them spoiled, disrespectful of authority, and self-centered. Will such children become easily adapted to life under a system that demands self-sacrifice and conformity? The answer to this question may be yes for China. But there are serious doubts of whether it can apply generally to LDCs. Other, less stringent, methods must be found to limit the rate of population growth.

India is the second most heavily populated nation of the world. The World Bank estimates that by A.D. 2000 its population will be nearly a billion and that by A.D. 2050 there will be 1.5 billion people living there. If this projection is accurate, it will then have become more heavily populated than China. The projection for China in A.D. 2050 is 1.45 billion. Population projections this far in the future are, of course, subject to a wide margin of error. In any event, however, it seems clear that India faces a tremendous population problem. Whether it will be as successful in meeting this problem with a multiparty democratic government as China will be with a totalitarian government is an interesting question.

One of the methods attempted by India was a massive compulsory sterilization program. In the years 1975-77 it is estimated that hundreds of thousands of people were sterilized against their will—often by brutal methods and under unsanitary conditions. This program faced such sharp internal criticism that it was largely abandoned.

Bangladesh, another country which is generally considered to be seriously overpopulated, is now considering a voluntary sterilization program coupled with financial incentives. Families with two or three living children could volunteer to be sterilized. If they accepted they would be given nonnegotiable bonds valued at $80 to $100, depending on the number of children they already had. These bonds would earn interest but they could not be cashed in for 12 years. However, prior to their maturity the bondholder could borrow up to 50 percent of the bond's value if the proceeds were used for purposes which would increase agricultural production. Such purposes might include poultry farming and fish culture or the purchase of fertilizer or irrigation pumps. Because of the operation of compound interest, the bonds would mature at the end of 12 years with a value of between $275 and $425. This money would then be a form of old-age security and would thus reduce the pressure on families to have children to provide for this need.

Although compulsory or voluntary incentives may help to reduce population growth in some cases, most population experts believe that indirect methods offer greater promise in the long run.

It has been observed that people with more income generally want fewer children. Therefore, the population problem is only one aspect of the larger problem of economic development. In that sense, the chapters of this book which follow all have an important—probably crucial—bearing on the solution of the population problem. Economic growth provides the means for expansion of educational opportunity. Better-educated families tend to be smaller families. Economic growth would also provide more resources for old-age security, thus reducing this factor causing large families.

Providing more educational opportunities for women would probably be the most effective method of reducing birth rates. In all countries, women who have completed primary school have fewer children than women with no formal education. As additional educational opportunities in the primary school level are provided, the number of children apparently decreases with the amount of education of the mother. A study of families in the Philippines, for example, reported average family size of more than six children for mothers with no schooling, five children where the mother had from one to three years of education, 3.5 children where the mother had four to six years of education, and only 2.5 where the mother was in school seven years or more. Similar studies in Kenya, Colombia, and Korea, though revealing a less striking relationship, all show a decrease in family size as the education of the wives increased.

Improving the educational opportunities for women is only one aspect—though a highly important one—of increasing the status of women. More and more women in the rich countries are employed full time outside the home. This has resulted in less time for the care of children and generally lower birth rates.

A recent demographic study has shown that similar results would obtain in LDCs even prior to the time that their income levels approach that of the more affluent countries. As the status of women advances, they tend to make increased use of contraceptives. Even more important, they tend to delay the age at which they marry. This extends the interval between generations and thus reduces population growth.

The average age at marriage for women in Bangladesh is 16. It is 25 in Sri Lanka. The total fertility rate in Sri Lanka was 3.2 in 1984. In Bangladesh it was 6.0. (The total fertility rate is the number of children born to the average woman during her reproductive years.) Factors other than the delay of the age of marriage may be partly responsible for these striking differences in the number of births, but the age at marriage is probably the most important one. Historical demographers have demonstrated that the decline of birth rates in Europe in the nineth century was also associated with the increase in the status of women.

Government social security programs would reduce the compulsion now felt by families in poor countries to have many children to provide for their needs in old age.

Conclusion

The Christian cannot help feeling ambivalent about attempts to solve the problems of poor countries by reducing the size of their families. Our Christian ethics emphasize the sacredness of human life. The Genesis account of the creation indicates that after God created man and woman he told them to "Be fruitful and multiply, and fill the earth and subdue it" (Genesis 1:28). The problem is that the earth is finite in size. The multiplication of the number of people using this finite space may directly work against the fulfillment of the second part of the command—to "subdue" the earth. Our problem is to find a happy medium between the multiplication of births and the effective subjection of the earth to God's purposes.

But the problem is made more difficult by the fact that pressure against the finite resources of the earth may result not only from the large birth rates prevailing in the poor nations; the wasteful consumption of the earth's resources by the rich nations is a more serious problem. The poor nations have used the occasion of world population conferences to remind the rich nations of this fact.

The most flagrant example of our wasteful consumption is our enormous military expenditure. But we also squander resources when we carelessly waste food or when we insist on consuming meat rather than grains and vegetables. As poorer nations become richer they no doubt will emulate the wasteful consumption habits of the rich. In the meantime, more concrete progress can be made if we voluntarily restrict our own wasteful consumption than if we preach population control to the poor nations.

Questions for further study and discussion

1. Why is the population of LDCs increasing more rapidly

than that of the rich countries?

2. Inasmuch as all human beings are of equal importance in the sight of God, do you think that it is appropriate for Christians to advocate measures which would reduce the rate of increase in population in poor countries?

3. Families in LDCs tend to regard a substantial number of children as security for parents in their old age. In the richer countries this function has largely been shifted from the family to private and governmental pension schemes. What are the gains and losses resulting from this shift?

4. What relevance, if any, does the Malthusian theory of population have for the LDCs of today?

5. Why is deforestation a problem for many LDCs? What steps can be taken to stop the trend toward deforestation?

6. What are some of the ethical issues involved in China's one-child policy? Do you think that it is probable that this policy will be used by other LDCs?

7. How can the status of women be improved in LDCs? How does improving the status of women in a country tend to cause a reduction in the average number of children per family?

8. Rich nations have criticized LDCs for having too many children. Poor nations have criticized rich nations for being too profligate in their habits of personal consumption and in their military expenditures. Which of these positions has the greater validity?

4

Agricultural and Rural Development

Agriculture is the dominant economic activity of the poorer countries. Approximately 70 percent of the population depends on agriculture. From 60 to 70 percent of the income of people in the LDCs is spent for food. Most of the nonagricultural activity in these economies is an outgrowth of agriculture. The governments depend on agriculture for a majority of their tax revenue. The improvement in agricultural output will, therefore, have a profound impact on the lives of most of the people living in these areas.

Many of the LDCs, recognizing that the rich countries are industrialized, feel that they can develop only through industrialization. In this they are following the example of socialist countries like the Soviet Union (and, in the initial stages of its communist revolution, China as well). The industrial development of Russia was achieved at the cost of tremendous suffering by the peasant class. Even today industrialization may be at the expense of adequate production of food. As is well known, Russia, once a part of the "bread basket of Europe," is now a large importer of grain.

The Industrial Revolution in Europe and the United States was preceded, or accompanied, by an agricultural revolution. As industry developed, the proportion of the population engaged in agriculture declined sharply, but the total output of food and other farm products continued to grow. In the United States less than 3 percent of the labor force is engaged in farming. But these farmers produce not only enough to feed the American population; they sell abroad one half or more of some of the crops they grow. Western Europe, once a heavy importer of food products, now has its "mountains of butter"—farm products in excess of the domestic needs.

Leaders of the LDCs are often understandably suspicious of Western experts who suggest that the initial stages of development should emphasize agriculture rather than industry. With the memory of their long period of political colonialism still fresh, they are not interested in having this followed by continued economic colonialism. They do not want to be the "hewers of wood and drawers of water" for the developed countries. They remember that the British attempted to dismantle the existing industries in colonial India (such as textiles and shipbuilding) in order to eliminate competition with British manufacturers of the same products. In fact, the British sought to agriculturalize India. In 1891, 61 percent of the population of India was working in agriculture. By 1921 it was 73 percent.

Chapter 6 will be devoted to a discussion of industrial development of LDCs. The present chapter will suggest some steps which should be taken to increase agricultural output. This is not to imply that agricultural production has been stagnant in recent years. During the 1950s worldwide agricultural output rose by 3.1 percent per year. The increase in the 1960s and the 1970s was less striking—2.6 percent in the 1960s and 2.2 percent in the 1970s. This decline was caused more by failures of agriculture in the planned socialist economies such as Russia and Eastern Europe than in the LDCs.

Fortunately, agricultural output in the LDCs in the 1980s took a dramatic turn for the better. The Chinese grain harvest was 315 million metric tons in 1979. Its 1984 grain harvest was a remarkable 407 million tons—an increase of nearly 30 percent in only five years. Wheat production more than doubled in this five-year period. India quadrupled its wheat production between 1967 and 1984. Once dependent on imports, it is now looking for an export market for some of its wheat. Rice production has more than doubled in Indonesia since 1973. It is now storing 3.5 million tons of rice at great cost. Bangladesh is now almost self-sufficient in grain. Indeed, the successes of food production in these great population centers is a major reason for the reduced demand for Iowa and Illinois corn and for Kansas wheat.

Land Tenure

Other things being equal, it has been demonstrated that farm production will be good when farmers have adequate incentives to produce. Farmers who own the land that they cultivate are more productive than are hired farm laborers. Tenant farmers who can retain for their own use or sale a substantial share of the crops they produce are more productive than tenants who must turn over much of their output to their landlords—especially to absentee landlords. The improvements in the production of grain in China and India can be attributed largely to incentive programs under way in these countries.

For most kinds of farm produce, the strength of American agriculture has been the family farm where the owner is also the operator. Land reform in Japan following World War II changed Japanese agriculture to an owner-operator system. Before World War II most Japanese farmers were tenants on large estates. Under American military occupation at the end of the war a thoroughgoing program of land reform was implemented. We usually think of General MacArthur as a conservative, but it was under his leadership that a truly radical redistribution of Japanese farmland was made. The land of the former large landowners was "sold" to the peasants who farmed the land, but the prices charged were prewar prices. Because of the depreciation of the yen during and immediately after the war, this meant that the land was virtually given to the operators. Since then the peasant class has been an important supporter of the conservative political leadership of Japan. Agricultural output has grown so that Japan is actually self-sufficient in rice.

Socialist countries have experimented with various new forms of land tenure. Their "ideal" has been the large (perhaps 10,000 acres) state farm. "Temporarily" they have allowed much of their farming to be on cooperative farms called collectives. These farms are usually smaller than the state farm. The farmers' income is more directly related to the output of their farms than is the case with the state farms. But the most productive parts of the agriculture in socialist economies have been the "private plots," where the farmers are free to produce what they want to produce and to dispose of their product as they choose. Even though these private plots occupy only about 4 percent of the Russia's arable land, they account for about 60 percent of Russia's production of potatoes and honey, more than 40 percent of its fruits, berries, and eggs, and 30 percent of its vegetables, milk, and meat. It seems clear that the Russian experience demonstrates that farmers who farm their own land as they see fit are more productive.

Yugoslavia's experience has been similar, as has that of Poland. Soon after the end of World War II the communist government in Warsaw sought to change the tenure of farm land into state farms or collectives. But the government found it impossible to get most of the farmers to accept this change. Today no less than 85 percent of Polish agriculture is carried on on privately owned farms.

Three-fourths of China's work force is employed in agriculture. In the early stages of the revolution which brought the communists to power, these farmers were organized into a system of large communes. China has now dismantled 56,000 of these communes. In their place they have developed a responsibility system whereby land is leased to farm households. After these households have met a fixed production target, they are free to sell any surplus in the open market. This has greatly stimulated agricultural production so that farm output has soared. Visitors to China today are impressed by the large private markets for farm products in the cities.

In spite of the failures of agriculture in socialist countries, socialist ideology persists. Karl Marx expected that socialism would triumph because of the work of the industrial proletariat.

He spent much of his life and wrote his greatest works in London—at that time the largest city in the world. He spoke with disdain of the "idiocy of rural life." But we know today that LDCs can develop most rapidly if their policies are dictated by pragmatic results rather than by the faulty judgment of urban theoreticians.

In many LDCs land ownership is still in the hands of the few. In Ethiopia, prior to the overthrow of Emperor Haile Selassie's government, much of the land was owned by the imperial family or by the Ethiopian Orthodox Church. Peasants who farmed the land had little incentive to innovate or to work hard. In other LDCs the land is still owned by the elite governing class or has been purchased by foreign multinational corporations.

These lessons from the developed countries and the socialist countries should be studied by LDCs. The ability and willingness of farmers to improve their own land and to profit personally from these improvements are often the critical factors in agricultural development. If the farmers own their own land, or feel secure in their tenancy, they are more likely to make the effort to drain it, irrigate it, or level it. Even where this is not at present feasible, landowners must take an active interest in cultivation. They must be prepared to invest, to innovate, and to improve the flow of inputs such as seeds, fertilizers, and pesticides. At the same time, tenancy should be stable, the rents charged should be moderate, and the tenant should receive a large enough share of the output to provide adequate initiative.

This is not to imply that these changes in the institutional framework of agriculture can be accomplished easily. The land must be surveyed. Frequently land titles must be adjudicated. Small and often widely scattered parcels of land must be consolidated. Inheritance traditions may need to be modified so that the farms can be maintained in the years ahead in viable units. Difficult though these tasks are to accomplish, they should be goals to guide policy.

Perhaps the most crucial problem in agricultural development is the political problem. Only strong governments can carry out the needed reforms. In a real sense, agricultural development is thus only one aspect of the need for political reform. The elite minorities who benefit from existing land tenure arrangements will certainly resist the needed changes. They may decry them as being communist-inspired and as part of a plot to extend Soviet influence throughout the third world. Shortsighted American political leaders may accept this line of argument and even supply the military equipment needed to thwart needed change. This is why it is so important that people in the rich countries understand the need for land reform so that agricultural production can be increased and hungry people fed.

Agricultural Research and Experimentation

When I visited the city of Saenz Pena in the Argentine Chaco, my hosts suggested that we visit a nearby agricultural experimentation station. On the surface it was not an impressive establishment. Its staff was relatively small. Its laboratories did not have the latest equipment. But it taught me an important lesson in the agricultural development. The Chaco is a poor part of Argentina. The experimentation being carried on there, though apparently primitive by North American standards, was entirely appropriate for the Argentine Chaco. The researchers were able to make the necessary careful analyses of soil types. New strains of seed and livestock were tested and adapted to local needs. Research into pest control and weed eradication was going forward. My visit to this experiment station underscored for me the importance of agricultural research.

For effective agricultural development to take place, economic research is also necessary. Improvements are possible if analyses are made of what is being done with the current agricultural output. How is farm income divided between consumption and reinvestment? What evidence is there that farmers would respond to greater economic opportunities? Generations of experience have made the peasants shrewd operators. Nevertheless, systematic observation may reveal ways in which they could do better, even using traditional techniques. Research may reveal that the peasants could be substantially more productive by trying new techniques.

Japan has demonstrated that it can engage in productive agriculture where the number of farmers per acre of cultivated land is almost 50 times as high as in the United States. Asian LDCs typically have high worker-land ratios. The Chinese use of hybrid rice has increased the average yield by about 30 percent. The per-acre yield of wheat and rice is now higher in China than in the United States. This is a result of the use of scientifically bred seeds, careful irrigation, and the use of organic fertilizer. The Japanese and Chinese experience may be more helpful to LDCs than the highly capitalistic labor-saving farm operations of the United States.

The Green Revolution

In the past most of the agricultural research in the tropical areas has been directed toward improving the yields and quality of export crops such as sugar, coffee, rubber, tea, bananas, and palm oil. Research in the production of cereals was conducted primarily for the benefit of the great grain-producing areas of the temperate climates. But in the last couple of decades, major breakthroughs have been made in techniques of producing wheat and rice in the tropical areas.

These changes have been referred to as the "Green Revolution." Norman Borlaug was awarded a Nobel Prize for his efforts in this behalf. In the mid-1960s new varieties of rice were developed by the International Rice Research Institute (IRRI) in the Philippines. Their work was supported in part by grants from the Rockefeller and Ford Foundations. A similar organization (with the acronym CIMMYT from its Spanish title) had earlier been working in Mexico to develop new varieties of wheat.

The new varieties of wheat were brought to India and Pakistan in 1966. By 1970-72 wheat production in India had doubled. Thereupon production stagnated because of a rust disease. But Indian scientists developed new varieties of wheat which resisted rust and which matured earlier. This caused production to increase again. By the late 1970s India had changed from being the second largest cereal importer (in 1966) to a country self-sufficient in wheat. In more recent years the production of rice, potatoes, and other nontraditional crops has expanded rapidly.

China, Turkey, and Pakistan quickly adopted the new wheat varieties and production increased significantly. Wheat production was scarcely known in Bangladesh a couple of decades ago. But by the early 1980s it was producing large amounts of wheat.

The new rice varieties were initially used mainly in the dry areas of southern and southeastern Asia where the farmers irrigated during the dry season. Rice varieties suitable for the monsoon areas were developed later. Under favorable conditions, double- and even triple-cropping was practiced and yields were enhanced.

Other crops are also important to tropical LDCs. Improved corn (maize) has been adopted in countries as diverse as China, Argentina, Zimbabwe, and Kenya. But some of the dramatically improved hybrids that have revolutionized corn production in the United States have not been successfully introduced in other countries where soil and climatic conditions are not suitable. Hybrid sorghums were brought to India in 1964. But they had to be adapted so that they could be more disease-resistant. People's reluctance to eat them also had to be overcome. Nevertheless, one-third of the rain-fed area of India is now being planted with these hybrids. They have also been used in northeastern China and in Latin America. In the latter countries they have been used primarily as cattle feed.

Sorghum is also being produced in increasing amounts in Mexico. It has proved to be easier to grow than corn. Furthermore, it brings a good price. Unlike the price of corn, which was for many years artificially held down by the Mexican government because it wanted to subsidize the urban tortilla eaters, the price of sorghum has been allowed to find its own very profitable level.

As a result, the producers of sorghum have benefited greatly. Companies which purchase it process it into feed for sale to livestock raisers. This has substantially increased livestock production, and the Mexicans are eating more meat.

But there are losses as well as gains. Many of the poor of Mexico have suffered by the change. They will eat corn but they don't eat sorghum and they can't afford to buy meat. So the hungry people of Mexico have less food than they had before. The government is using some of its precious foreign exchange to buy corn from abroad. It is also increasing the price it pays for domestically grown corn.

The Mexican experience with sorghum is another illustration of the differing results of the Green Revolution. It has improved the lives of millions of farmers in the poor countries. But it has been criticized because it has not benefited a still larger number of the poorest farmers in many countries. In Mexico the farmers with the poorest land found that they could not raise sorghum. In some cases the problem was an inadequate supply of rainfall and irrigation; elsewhere it was poor flood control. Sometimes the poorest farmers did not have the resources to buy the expensive seeds and fertilizers which were required. In some countries regional research was not available to adapt the new seeds to the local soil and climatic conditions. Sometimes the problem was one of providing adequate transportation and marketing facilities. Nevertheless, on the average, food production per capita has expanded significantly. We will look at some of these statistics at the end of this chapter.

Agricultural Extension Services

The results of agricultural research must be communicated to the farmers. This requires an effective extension service. Unfortunately, some LDCs now have very inadequate field staffs. In some countries the extension agents are viewed as tax collectors—natural enemies. Another difficulty is that extension agents are usually educated civil servants from the city. They may not want to dirty their hands in the field. The most effective agents are those who are willing to work alongside the farmer. Farmers will be most easily convinced if they can be shown the successful experience of their friends and neighbors.

Some extension agents give most of their attention to the

large and wealthy farmers, neglecting the small farmers who may be most in need of help. The agents may neglect women farmers even though they may have exclusive responsibility for the production of some food crops. In other places women do all but the initial land clearing and heavy plowing. Difficulties such as these have caused some authorities to conclude that extension service which has done so much to improve the output of American farms has thus far not contributed much to the improvement of LDC agriculture. Certainly much more remains to be done.

Peasants in LDCs are often poorly educated and sometimes are apparently inhibited by a blind conservatism. But in part they may hesitate to experiment with changed methods because of the fear of failure. Failure may mean disaster for families which already are producing at the subsistence level. Rational risk-aversion may be a stronger factor than blind conservatism. Some kind of insurance against this risk may be required if the poorest farmers are really to be helped.

Adequate Inputs

Improved agricultural methods developed by careful research and communicated to farmers with effective extension services are still not going to be helpful unless farmers have available improved inputs. These may include items such as seeds, fertilizers, pesticides, and herbicides. They may in some cases involve the use of simple machinery.

Machinery has not been widely used in many LDCs because LDCs usually have more workers than they can employ effectively. However, items such as stationary threshers, water pumps, and mills are so much superior to human labor that they may find increased use. There are scarcely any tractors in Bangladesh, but irrigation pumps are widely used. In central Thailand the second rice crop must be planted before the first crop can be threshed by the traditional buffalo-treading methods. In such cases the need for speed justifies the use of mechanical rice threshers.

Agricultural output can be increased greatly by the use of fertilizer. The high yields of farms in the rich countries owe much to heavy fertilization. However, now that the rich countries are already using so much fertilizer, world agricultural output could be expanded more by concentrating additional fertilizer on the fields of the LDCs.

Historically, animal manure has been the most important form of fertilization. Not only does it provide necessary plant nutrients; it also improves the structure of the soil and adds to the ability of the soil to retain water. However, in many poor countries farmers use animal manure for many other purposes and the farmers apparently consider it economical to do so. In some countries it is used to plaster the walls or floors of their homes. In an Ethiopian village one can see large piles of manure chips which have been gathered from the fields and stored until they are used to provide fuel.

Human waste ("night soil") is a very important form of fertilizer, especially in the heavily populated areas of Asia. Typically, the waste is collected from small buckets under the toilets in homes and stored in larger tanks in the fields. It is then applied to the land where the crops are grown, usually at critical periods during the growth process. Since this is obviously a labor-intensive operation, countries such as Japan have recently begun to use increasing amounts of chemical fertilizer as a substitute. The extensive use of night soil may also contribute significantly to the spread of certain diseases.

When my family was living in Japan we hesitated to use lettuce or other fresh vegetables in our salads. We feared that the leafy vegetables had been fertilized with night soil and that we would get amoebic dysentery from eating them. However, Melvin J. Loewen of the World Bank staff reports: "When night soil is allowed to lie in open air for six months the pathogens are dead and the fertilizer can be used safely even in vegetable gardens. China got into trouble for a while when it used the night soil too quickly. Now this source of fertilizer is in such great demand that we recently had an 'incident' in Shanghai when the city wanted to extend its modern water-borne sewerage system. The farmers objected to this deprivation of a ready fertilizer."

In LDCs chemical fertilizers have been used in the past

mainly to enhance the production of their export crops. In the past couple of decades, however, fertilizer use has increased eightfold. The rapid increase in grain yields since 1950 is a result not only of better seeds and irrigation but also of the large increase in the use of fertilizer. Higher oil prices since the 1970s have sharply increased the costs of commercial fertilizer. This should lead to increasing emphasis on the use of animal manure and on the use of legume crops which add atmospheric nitrogen to the soil.

In much of Asia, North Africa, and the Middle East, irrigation—which can permit double- and even triple-cropping—has markedly increased agricultural yields. The additional jobs created by the building of these new irrigation projects have often benefited the whole economy of the region.

Since 1960 irrigated areas have increased at a rate of 2.2 percent per year. This represents more than 350 million acres of irrigated land. Much of this is in China and India. But irrigation projects are expensive. If they require large canal schemes and storage reservoirs, they may cost as much as $1000 per acre. They are still more expensive if the people building them are inexperienced in construction or if the materials must be imported. Effective projects also obviously require an adequate supply of ground and surface water—a vital resource which, unfortunately, is often absent in the poorest countries.

More modest private irrigation methods should also be used. Open wells and tubewells have made it possible for millions of small farmers to irrigate. Often their use is supported by the government through public credit and rural electrification. But the initial investment required for simple pumps and tubewells is much smaller than for the big irrigation schemes. Furthermore, they require little administrative skill. They should make possible significant increases in agricultural productivity.

Finally, more attention should be given to reducing the loss of crops through disease and through predators both during the growing season and when the crops are stored. Some estimates place this loss at as high as 30 or 40 percent. Pesticides have been widely used and with good results. But there is increased concern about undesirable side-effects of some of them. They can deposit potentially harmful residues. They can cause outbreaks of secondary pests or destroy natural enemies. If land is abundant relative to farm labor (a condition not often found in LDCs), herbicides may also be used to increase production.

Improving Marketing

We have already noted that most agricultural production in LDCs is subsistence production. However, as production expands, additional marketing facilities must be developed. Urban consumers must be supplied with food; some of the output may be sold abroad. But this will not happen unless there are intermediaries who can buy, sell, store, transport, and sometimes process the farmers' product. This will not take place automatically without planning. But the experience in West Africa since the turn of the century in the marketing of cocoa, peanuts, and cotton shows that farmers generally respond quickly to market opportunities. The production of cocoa beans alone in West Africa has now reached over 1 million tons a year. This has supplied 70 percent of the world's market. It is the best cash crop ever grown there.

Some agricultural products are produced for export through multinational firms located in the country. Although this provides foreign exchange, it may not significantly increase the standard of living of the poorer people of the third world. Instead, the benefits may go to an elite within the country. The poorer people are even disadvantaged if the land used to produce the export product is more urgently needed to provide basic food for the poor.

Trends in Food Production in LDCs

Is food production in LDCs increasing? The World Bank has reported that the average food production per capita in the 36 low income countries was 16 percent higher in 1982-84 than it was eight years earlier. In the 60 middle income countries the improvement was 4 percent. But the pattern was by no means uniform in the countries in each of these categories. Sri Lanka showed a growth of 25 percent. Production in Somalia, on the other hand, declined by 31 percent and in Ghana by 27 percent. Significantly, production in some of the most heavily populated countries expanded—in India by 10 percent and in China by 28 percent. This comparison overstates China's accomplishment. China's production in the mid-1970s was abnormally low because of the excesses of the Cultural Revolution. The reported improvement is, therefore, less significant than if normal political conditions had existed 12 years ago.

Among the low-income countries, the countries in sub-Sahara Africa seem in general to have fared the worst. The U.S. Department of Agriculture recently reported that the per capita grain production in Africa declined from 142 kilograms per person in 1966 to 117 in 1984. The production fluctuated from year to year, but in all of the years 1966-84 it was below 180 kilograms, the amount considered necessary for meeting a subsistence level.

Africa has long been plagued by unfavorable climatic conditions. But Africa's problems also stem from inefficiencies in production and marketing. Ghanaians recently could buy imported corn more cheaply than locally grown corn. Burkina Faso (Upper Volta) has beef to sell. But neighboring Côte d'Ivoire (Ivory Coast) can buy its beef (frozen) more cheaply from Europe. This is caused in part by subsidies paid producers in the countries of the European Economic Community. But it also stems from inefficiencies in Burkina Faso. Local palm oil used in the manufacture of soap in Ghana is reported to be 50 percent more expensive than imported tallow.

How Christians Can Help

How can Christians help improve agricultural output in LDCs? In chapter 5 I will show how Christian young people from the United States and Canada made a significant contribution to the improvement of secondary education in some LDCs. When I was in Dar es Salaam, Tanzania, a veteran missionary spoke appreciatively of the work of these young Christian teachers from abroad. But he suggested that what was more urgently needed was young agricultural experts.

Such an assignment would require a higher level of preparation and would also require a commitment to a longer period of service than is expected of teachers. Most of the teachers went for only three-year terms. Some of them had to make intensive preparation in the French language before they went, but most of them taught in English. Many of them had no academic preparation beyond the baccalaureate degree.

To give significant help in agriculture, young persons from abroad would have to have specialized training in tropical agriculture. Furthermore, they would have to have additional study to adapt this background to the special soil and climatic conditions in the area where they serve. Above all, they would need to have a knowledge of the language of the people they were serving and a willingness to live and work at their side. This is asking a lot, but it is not an impossible objective for which to strive.

I conclude this chapter by quoting at length from a letter I received from Jon Nofziger, Mennonite Central Committee (MCC) volunteer in Haiti. His experience in seeking to promote agricultural development in that poor country illustrates much of what I have been saying in this chapter.

> One of the most urgent tasks of service to humanity is to help villagers grow more food on their land.
>
> Experts report that land on a slope of 30 percent or more should not be tilled; rather, left in grass or tree cover. In Haiti most land has a slope of over 30 percent. With continued tillage this soil is exposed to further erosion. One farmer I met was convinced that the rocks in his field (perhaps 50 percent slope and years of cultivation) were growing since they were "bigger this year than last." As the soil is washed away, crop yields decrease and farmers are forced to till more land, if obtainable, to reap the needed harvests to feed themselves and their families. Obviously some basic education is called for, nothing too theoretical, just helping piece the puzzles with simple pragmatic means.
>
> We began a project to reduce soil erosion. The primary goal was to get trees on the hillsides. Yet trees could not be ends in themselves; they needed to be included in education, agricultural systems, and marketing to aid in erosion control and ultimately be a means of increased food production. The project

faced limitations from its genesis, in that planting trees was a very foreign concept, and some farmers couldn't spare land needed for food to plant trees. The first two years were devoted to convincing and encouraging people of the need . . . to include trees into their traditional agriculture, not replace it. We began by planting borders around the fields and/or small areas with solid plantings. This not only got trees planted, but allowed for some concepts of managing trees—principles of thinning and pruning to receive desired yields for fuel wood, posts, or lumber.

After the second year, trees were selling themselves with quick tangible results. Demand far outpaced supply. This increased interest led people to start small nurseries for their own needs. With this given, other issues could now . . . be presented. At a meeting, the question was posed, "Each year we harvest less and food prices are increasing; what can we do?" After two hours of discussion, an answer came forth—erosion needed to be controlled.

Following that meeting, MCC staff decided to aid this process by offering technical assistance. It was realized that a patient schedule would be needed. The primary step would be to teach benefits and techniques of various contour barriers and how one finds the contour along a hillside. A demonstration was given on the construction and uses of an A-frame level (a low technology tool using three sticks, three nails, piece of string, and a rock). Participants were asked to construct one for their use and the group would visit another's fields to work together putting into action the new techniques. This gave the area eight demonstration plots and lots of questions on what had been done.

Let me emphasize the idea of working together. In many cultures, when one breaks the norm of traditional practice, pressure and ridicule are directed at that person. Often this pressure leads that person back to the norm. A group working together can offer the support and encouragement needed to see a new practice through the trial phase.

Contour barriers were constructed of plant residue and/or rocks. This left the plots clean and ready to plant when rains began. Remembering that arresting erosion was the main goal, concrete results were seen after the first rain. I measured up to four inches of soil accumulated behind the ramps. These ramps also broke the velocity of water running downhill and allowed for infiltration to occur, thus increasing soil moisture. The reasons for selecting plant residue and rocks as material—other than availability—would be given in future lessons. We didn't want to overload the farmers with new ideas, especially ideas that would take several seasons to show results.

The reason for using plant material to construct the contour barriers was to keep organic matter in the soil. Burning the fields before planting, as is practiced, rapes the soil of valuable nutrients and humus which is critical in the ability of the soil to retain moisture. Available water is the limiting factor in early stages of plant development. With the rocks gathered, hoeing is facilitated and weed control becomes effective. This also frees water to be used by the crops.

The secondary step was to show farmers how to increase soil fertility. We could now explain what extra benefits the contour ramps were giving. Now that trees were accepted a new idea could be tried. This was to seed trees along the barriers, to be managed as a hedge and so not reduce the land area for crops. This technique of a living barrier would develop a root system to stabilize the soil and yield valuable leaf litter for decomposition and manural value. (Reports on the species used say that six units of dried leaf matter has the same nutritional value as one unit of commercial fertilizer, but at no cost.) This species chosen was a member of the legume family, which forms a symbiotic relationship with bacteria that can take atmospheric nitrogen and make it available to plants. Other uses of the trimmings could be animal fodder or fuel.

This was the result of the program after three years. We have developed a series of lessons on how to increase crop yields. The series runs for three years and involves learning or practicing only one or two new techniques each year. The first year has been spent in controlling erosion by constructing contour barriers and explaining how to increase organic matter in the soil. The second year includes trials with planting systems and plant densities. The third, seed selection and storage, conducting exploration of own ideas (trial plots with control) and how to present one's acquired knowledge and experience to others.

Our program assumed that before crop production could be increased, one needed soil. Thus, erosion control was the obvious first. In all cases, though, I would suggest that Christians can best aid the effort to provide adequate food in poorer countries by: (1) working on a small scale, introduce only one or two new ideas per year; (2) advancing proven methods that don't require large energy expenditures, either manual or financial; (3) having results easily and readily measurable; (4) proper timing: don't attempt something new in a traditional busy period, (i.e., planting or harvesting); (5) promoting people to work together in groups; (6) letting nationals assume ownership.

Conclusion

Agriculture is still the largest and most important industry. For all except a few highly specialized economies, improvement in agricultural production is the most significant single aspect of general economic growth.

Questions for further study and discussion

1. Why are leaders in LDCs suspicious when people in the rich countries emphasize agricultural development as the most important first step toward general economic development?

2. Why are land tenure systems often of crucial importance in agricultural development?

3. What are the strengths and weaknesses of the Green Revolution?

4. What are the strengths and weaknesses of agricultural extension services as carried on in LDCs?

5. If the present world consumption of fertilizer were shifted so that a larger share were used by the poor countries and a smaller share by the rich countries, total world agricultural output would be enhanced. Discuss the factors that militate against such a shift and suggest ways of promoting it.

6. Irrigation expands agricultural output. What are the costs which it entails and what are the limitations to the further development of irrigation projects?

7. Agricultural production has expanded in most parts of the

world other than in Africa. At the same time, population growth in Africa has been larger than on any other continent. Why has agricultural output in Africa lagged?

8. In what specific ways could we North American Christians encourage young people in our churches to view foreign service devoted to the improvement of agriculture as a lifetime calling?

5

Human Development: Education and Health

In 1960 less than 10 percent of the adult population of many poor countries could read and write. By 1980 the literacy rate of the 34 poorest countries had increased to 52 percent. This was a remarkable achievement, even though, of course, it was still much below the 99 percent rate which we now take for granted in the rich countries.

In 1960 the average life expectancy at birth in the 36 poorest countries was only 42 years. In some of these countries it was as low as 29 years. By 1984 this had increased to 60 years. Although again this was a distinct improvement, it was much below the 76 years in the rich countries.

Adult literacy and life expectancy are only two of the measures of educational and health development. They tell us much of the quality of human capital available in a country. They are important measures because if they are low they contribute to other factors that affect the quality of life in the poorer countries. It will be the purpose of this chapter to discuss various features of educational and health development.

Economic development is accompanied by an increase in the use of capital in production. Although many immediately think of capital as factory buildings and machinery necessary for industrialization, it may well be that more significant progress can be made if attention is given first to the improvement of human capital. Japan is one of the most thoroughly developed countries of the world. It is now highly industrialized. But compared with other countries, its human capital was superior even before the industrialization process began. More than a century ago Emperor Meiji told his people that they "should go out into all the world and seek knowledge wherever it may be found." Investment in human capital must come before maximum returns can be expected from other forms of capital investment.

The Costs and Benefits of Educational Expenditure

What are the costs and the benefits of educational expenditure? It is obvious that school buildings must be constructed, teachers hired, and educational books and other supplies purchased. In the tropical areas where many of the poor countries are located, educational programs are sometimes carried out in an open field supported by little more than a chalkboard hanging from the limb of a tree. Even where school buildings are constructed they can be adequate even when they are very simple and relatively inexpensive. Usually there need be no expenditures for heating equipment and fuel. Many of the rooms need not have glass windows. They require a substantial roof to provide protection from the hot sun and the rain, but the side walls may not have glass windows but only wide open spaces to bring in ventilation and light. The walls may be no more costly than mud bricks that have been dried and baked in the sun. The roof may be corrugated metal, but if it is thatched, it will provide more protection from the hot rays of the sun.

The expenditure for teachers is also often minimal, but greater educational progress could be made if they were better qualified and more adequately paid. In some of the poorer countries, elementary teachers for the young children have only five or six years of education themselves and no training in educational methods. Such teachers are poorly paid and so only a relatively small educational budget is required to employ them. But the effectiveness of the educational system could certainly be improved if the quality of the teaching were enhanced. This will require a larger financial outlay.

Educational equipment and supplies often consist of simple student desks, a very minimum of books, and a chalkboard. Teachers lecture to the children who copy the lectures into their own notebooks. Again, better results could be attained if more money were invested in the improvement of educational equipment and supplies.

It is sometimes not recognized by outside "experts" that the greatest cost of education is the time spent by the teachers and especially by the pupils. But these costs are understood by the parents of the children. They are often the major factor contributing to the reluctance of parents to have their children go to school. School-age children are needed to care for their younger siblings and to contribute to the planting, cultivating, and harvesting of subsistence farm crops. Although lower birth rates would reduce this pressure, lower birth rates are not likely to be achieved until the educational level is increased. But increasing the educational level entails additional costs which are burdensome to a subsistence economy. Help from the outside will make these additional costs less onerous.

The costs of improved education are much more than balanced by the benefits realized. The benefits are not merely economic. But the economic rate of return is high. In a study of 11 countries where the adult literacy rate was below 50 percent, the World Bank found that the rate of return was 27.3 percent for primary education, 17.2 percent for secondary education, and 12.1 percent for higher education. I will discuss later the implications for policy of the lower rates of return for the higher educational levels. Here I will refer to the benefits of primary education.

Primary Education

Studies made in such diverse areas as Brazil, Kenya, Malaysia, Nepal, and South Korea showed that, on the average, farmers who had completed four years of primary education were able to produce 13.2 percent more than those who had not been to school. This would suggest that primary education is important even for subsistence farmers.

Primary education is even more obviously important for persons who are employed by government agencies and by modern enterprises in the urban areas. Such people certainly should be literate and able to do simple arithmetic. But primary schooling also promotes disciplined work habits and enables students to profit from on-the-job training, particularly if they are to do other than purely routine tasks.

In 1983 in the 35 poorest countries, 91 percent of the primary school age-group were reported to be enrolled in school. But in every one of these countries the proportion was lower for females than for males. This obviously presents a serious ethical problem of equity. But it has many other significant effects as well. Education of girls may be the most important investment a country can make in insuring its future economic growth and welfare. This is true even for girls who do not enter the paid labor force.

In chapter 3, I pointed out that education of girls usually delays the age of their marriage. This means that they are likely to have fewer children. Furthermore, they are more likely to be aware of the availability of contraceptives and to use them. The consequent reduction in the birth rate may reduce population pressure and thus enhance living standards.

Studies in Kenya, Colombia, and Bangladesh show that infant and child death rates are lower among families where the mother has had primary education. Furthermore, for families at the same income level, the greater the education afforded the mothers, the better the nutrition provided the children. These findings, too, have long-range implications. Malnutrition not only stunts physical growth; it also often causes brain damage and thus militates against future economic development.

One of the lasting contributions made by Christian missionaries in Japan in the latter part of the nineteenth century was the establishment of schools for women and girls. After the Meiji Restoration in 1868, the government placed a high priority on education. But the governmental focus was largely on the education of men and boys. The Christian missionaries corrected this discrimination by establishing schools for the other sex.

I noted in chapter 2 that LDCs ordinarily have less equal distribution of income than developed countries. Expenditures for primary education tend to redistribute income toward the poor in the country. This is in contrast to expenditures for secondary and higher education. At this stage of their development, very few of the poorest people qualify for secondary and higher education. Consequently, government expenditure for education at these higher levels may in the initial stages of development result in even greater inequities. A study in Malaysia in 1974 reported public expenditures per household for the poorest 20 percent of the population and for the richest 20 percent. At the primary education level such expenditures were three times as high for the poorest as for the richest. At the postsecondary level the situation was reversed. It was 15 times as high for the richest 20 percent as for the poorest.

Primary education has a value that goes beyond the purely economic—important though the economic may be to development. Just as people receive noneconomic benefits from listening to great music and looking at great works of art, there are also noneconomic benefits resulting from all levels of formal educational activity. People who have associated with others of their own age in the learning process are more likely to be receptive to new ideas. They learn to accept discipline. These qualities tend to make them more productive economically. In the classroom they may also develop self-confidence and tolerance and learn civic responsibility. These qualities, though political or personal in nature, may also contribute ultimately to economic performance.

Secondary Education

Secondary education has been a serious bottleneck in some developing countries, especially in Africa. When the former Belgian Congo became Zaire, there was only a handful of secondary school graduates in the entire country. In some countries secondary education was reserved for the elite.

One of the problems in many countries is that secondary education involves removing the pupils from their village and placing them away from home in a central location. This is necessary so that the total enrollment is sufficiently large to make a secondary school feasible.

Establishing centrally located high schools, however, presents some language problems. The native language which is adequate as a language of instruction for a primary school in a village is not suitable for a secondary school where the students are often drawn from several language groups. Furthermore, educational materials at the secondary level are usually not available in the languages of the various ethnic groups. In Africa the solution is generally to offer secondary instruction in English or French. English is used in secondary and higher education in Ethiopia, even though the colonial power which once held the country was Italy. English is used in many of the East African countries and in such West African countries as Ghana and Nigeria, which were formerly British colonies. French is used in Zaire, Côte d'Ivoire (Ivory Coast), and other former Belgian or French colonies. In any event, however, going to a secondary school means studying in a foreign language.

Despite this difficulty, there continues to be an urgent need for secondary school graduates. They are required for employment in government service and in industry. They are obviously needed before a country can develop a university or other postsecondary educational system. Although primary school teachers are not always secondary school graduates, the primary schools could be greatly improved if their faculties were at least this well educated.

Actually, some secondary schools are teacher training "colleges." In this respect the situation in some LDCs today is not appreciably different from that of the United States 50 or 60 years ago. At that time U.S. "normal schools" were designed to prepare primary school teachers. Many present-day American state colleges and universities have developed out of the normal schools of a halfcentury ago.

In some countries secondary schools were established by missionary societies and other private groups. Initially these schools were heavily subsidized by churches or philanthropic organizations. The first buildings were often built by gifts from abroad. The faculty were largely expatriate personnel who were financially supported by the overseas churches or agencies which sent them. However, pupils were sometimes charged a nominal tuition. As the schools expanded new facilities were provided by local or national government funds. The educational budget also included funds for teachers' salaries.

When the countries of Africa received their political independence, two other developments occurred simultaneously. In the first place, the new national leaders recognized the need for expanding the size of the secondary education programs. This meant constructing more school buildings and employing additional secondary school teachers.

In the second place, the new governments needed personnel for the government offices. Under colonial rule most of the civil servants had been expatriates from the country exercising the colonial rule. With independence, these people returned to their home countries. In some cases the largest group of educated people remaining in the country were the nationals who were teachers in the secondary schools. Many of these people left the classroom to assume the civil service jobs vacated by the expatriate personnel. But this worked against the achievement of the first objective—providing sufficient staff to expand the size of the secondary school program.

In the early 1960s the Mennonite Central Committee established the Teachers Abroad Program (TAP) as its contribution toward meeting this need. College graduates—often with no previous teaching experience—were sent to Africa and, in smaller numbers, to some other developing areas as well. They usually served for three-year terms and at times were reappointed for additional terms. The educational budgets of the host countries provided their travel expenses, their living expenses and a small cash allowance.

With the growth of university programs in the LDCs in the 1970s fewer TAP teachers were sent to those countries. LDCs were now in a position to provide their own teaching personnel.

I have referred to the MCC-TAP program only as an illustration. There were other programs which also provided teachers.

One of these was the Teachers for East Africa (TEA) under the auspices of Teachers College of Columbia University. In some countries the U.S. Peace Corps served similar needs. Canadian and European governments and private agencies also contributed personnel through various programs.

I have emphasized the importance of secondary school graduates in providing teachers for schools and personnel for government service and for modern industry. But they also were needed for service as health workers and agricultural extension officials. As their skills were developed, they could also serve as technicians, managers, and administrators. These skills can also be acquired through on-the-job training. But the secondary schools can provide the initial impetus and can develop the climate where subsequent on-the-job training can be most fruitful.

Higher Education

University educational programs are also the goal of many LDCs—even of small ones. Such education is very costly especially where the number of students available for a given department is limited. A World Bank study showed that the countries of Sub-Saharan Africa were spending 100 times as much per student for postsecondary education as for elementary education. In the Middle East and North Africa the ratio was 17 times. In other developing areas it was eight or nine times. In contrast, the ratio in the rich countries of the world was only two times. One is tempted to say that university education is just too expensive for the smaller and poorer LDCs.

An important reason for the high cost of university education is that universities in some of the smaller LDCs had too many departments and tried to offer too many fields of specialized study.

In 1963-64 I served on the faculty of Haile Selassie University in Ethiopia. At that time the total enrollment in all of the schools of that university was less than 1,200 students. But the university had 13 deans of its various colleges. Some of these colleges at that time were only in the development stage and had no students. They have, of course, grown significantly in the past couple of decades. But some of the constituent colleges still remain too small to be economically viable.

In the early stages following independence in East Africa some thoughtful leaders had the vision for a "University of East Africa." A portion of this university would be located in each of three countries: Kenya, Uganda, and Tanzania. Undergraduate four-year degrees would be offered on all of its campuses. But at the graduate level, the campus at Kampala in Uganda might specialize in medical education; the one in Nairobi, Kenya, in engineering and science; and the unit in Dar es Salaam, Tanzania, in business and law. But the vision was not realized. Each campus preferred to develop graduate level specialties in all these areas and in others as well. This is a costly and inefficient use of higher education resources.

The need for university-educated people could be met if faculty members were brought in from abroad or if students were sent abroad 'for study. The Fulbright Program of the United States and the American Agency for International Development (AID) contributed many faculty members for service in LDCs. The latter usually worked through contracts between a specific American university and a new university in a developing country. Canada and many European countries had similar programs.

Many students from LDCs went abroad for their undergraduate and graduate education. Some went to the Soviet Union or China, as well as to European and North American institutions. In 1972, 85,000 students from LDCs were enrolled in American colleges and universities. Of these, 16,000 were sponsored by the U.S. government. Approximately 26,000 students from LDCs— all of them governmentally sponsored—were enrolled in Soviet bloc countries. By 1982, 243,000 students from LDCs were enrolled in American colleges and universities, but only 10,000 of these were governmentally sponsored. The number of LDC students in Soviet bloc schools had grown to 93,000.

Certainly when these international students return to their home countries they will make a tremendous impact on the development of their national economies. But their experience abroad is not without its problems. Most of the international students come from the more well-to-do families in their home countries. The education they receive abroad tends to aggravate existing inequities in the distribution of wealth and income in the countries from which they came. Furthermore, if students spend four years in an undergraduate institution abroad and then remain abroad from three to five years to gain additional specialized training, there is a real danger that they will not return to their home countries. If they do return, they might have difficulty in adjusting to life back home. They will likely prefer to live in the cities where the amenities of life more nearly compare with those to which they had become accustomed abroad as international students. This tends to create a surplus of educated personnel in the major cities even though acute shortages still remain in the provincial areas. Some seek employment in international agencies related to the United Nations. Some become a part of what we call the "brain drain."

Brain Drain

It is estimated that nearly 500,000 technical and professional workers were admitted to the United States between 1969 and 1979. Nearly half of these persons came from Asia. Three-fourths of them came from LDCs. The brain drain caused Sudan to lose 44 percent of her scientists, engineers, and medical practitioners. In 1976-78, 17 percent of the total emigrants from Bangladesh were professional and technical personnel. Certainly this contributed to a shortage of people with these skills in Bangladesh. In some other countries, such as India and Egypt, the number of professional persons migrating was even larger. But they represented a smaller percentage of the total group of skilled persons in the countries from which they came.

The governments of LDCs are understandably concerned about the loss of their skilled workers. Often they have provided all or part of the costs of their education. Governments of LDCs still need to continue to fund some travel expenses for their skilled people going to developed countries for study and research. This will facilitate the growth of specialized learning and the transfer of technical skills from the richer to the poorer nations.

But it should be recognized that when these skilled workers emigrate to the richer countries, the governments lose the opportunity to tax the incomes of the emigrants. In most cases it was the richer elites who benefited from the education and should have been most able to pay taxes. It is estimated that the professional immigrants admitted to the U.S. from 1969-79 probably had aggregate earnings of about $6 billion. If the sending countries could have imposed a 10 percent tax on these earnings it would have produced $600 million. This would be the equivalent of about 13 percent of the official development assistance from the United States to these countries in 1979.

International students have made a splendid contribution to the intellectual atmosphere of many liberal arts colleges in the developed countries. However, as undergraduate education becomes more readily available in LDCs, most students who now come to undergraduate colleges in developed countries should rather receive this education in their home countries. They should delay coming to the more developed countries until they are ready for their graduate and specialized studies. This would reduce the total cost per student appreciably. And it would mean a shorter period of absence from their home countries. This would also make it easier to reenter their home countries and cause them to be less likely to seek to emigrate to the developed countries.

Meeting the Costs of Education

Education is costly. LDCs usually need to devote a larger share of their GNP for education than the richer nations do. The World Bank reported that in 1983 the low-income countries spent on the average 4.7 percent of their gross national product on education. The contrasting figure for the U.S. is only 1.9 percent and for Canada 3.6 percent. Governments of LDCs apparently recognize the crucial significance of education in their development.

Unfortunately, for the low-income countries, the 4.7 percent in 1983 was a sharp decrease from 12.7 percent spent in 1972. The main reason for this decrease is that the percentage of GNP spent for on their armed forces grew from 17.2 in 1972 to 19.5 in 1983. Inasmuch as these figures are still below the 23.7 percent of GNP which the U.S. spent on its armed forces in 1983, an American should probably hesitate to be too critical of the low-income countries' priorities. Both groups spend entirely too much on armaments, which in economic terms is essentially unproductive. One can't eat a tank, and it must be an uncomfortable vehicle to use for a visit to one's aunt!

The World Bank also gives figures for education and military expenditures made by 40 lower-middle-income countries. They offer a striking contrast to the pattern in the 36 poorest countries.

Educational expenditures absorb a higher share of GNP and military expenditures a lower share in the middle-income group than in the low-income countries. The percentage of GNP spent for education in the middle group is 12.1 percent (compared with 4.7 percent for the poorest countries) and the percentage spent upon armed forces is 11.4 percent (compared to 19.5 percent by the poorest). Furthermore, whereas in the poorest group of countries the share of GNP spent for education fell between 1972 and 1983 while the share for armaments was rising, in the middle-income group the reverse was happening— the share for armaments was falling more than the share for education.

The obvious conclusion is that though education is expensive for the poorest countries, it is not as expensive as building and maintaining their armed forces. The poorest countries—like the rich—should reorder their priorities away from the mad military race and toward improving the minds and skills of their people.

But there are some ways in which countries can economize on educational expenditure without reducing the quality of education. Correspondence courses are relatively inexpensive and have significantly reduced the cost of teacher training and secondary and higher education. The Air-Correspondence

High School in Korea has provided secondary education at about one-fifth the cost of traditional schools. As they study these students can continue to earn a living. The experience of Brazil, Kenya, and the Dominican Republic has also demonstrated that correspondence courses are effective and especially appropriate for people in remote areas.

Vocational Education

It is generally agreed that one of the crucial developments in education in the United States in the nineteenth century was the passage of the Morrill Act in 1862. This provided for land grants to states for the establishment of colleges for the "agricultural and mechanical arts." The developing countries of the twentieth century may well profit from this example. We think of education in the arts and the humanities as being the mark of the cultivated intellect. Indeed, they are tremendously important. But some degree of economic development needs to occur before the arts and the humanities can flourish. Vocational education is a vital concomitant of economic development.

It is important that the vocational education not be too narrowly specialized. Rather, education in skills with a wide variety of applications will make the student better qualified to benefit from later on-the-job training or short-term courses. These often provide training that is not "once and for all time," but rather that will have to be repeated as the country develops and job opportunities change.

Is it possible to overeducate? We have all heard of the arts graduate in India who is either unemployed or can find only menial work. In India engineers seem to be in surplus. Unemployment among secondary school graduates is a still more serious problem in some countries. Often these graduates tend to migrate to the cities and to insist on white-collar jobs which the economy is not yet able to provide.

Unemployment statistics in developing countries are notably unreliable. It is probable that the open unemployment of secondary school graduates (and even of secondary school dropouts) is no more serious than the disguised unemployment which would have been the alternative for these people in the rural areas from which they came. However, this group may be highly active politically. Their political volatility can be a threat to the stability of the government and this in turn can have a deleterious effect on economic development.

Where unemployment exists among the educated young people in a developing country, the government officials should not quickly decide to close schools and reduce educational expenditure. Instead, they might be advised to consider: (1) making modifications in the school curricula so as to seek to provide education in skills for which there is a visible demand (2) improving the counseling service and vocational information for high school students so that they can avoid unrealistic expectations but rather choose courses of study which will prepare them for jobs which are available and (3) making teaching jobs in primary and secondary education more attractive so as to draw more of the educated labor force in that direction. It is unfortunate, indeed, if university graduates languish in unemployment in the cities when at the same time there is a severe shortage of teachers in the rural areas.

Health

At the beginning of this chapter I pointed out that human capital can be improved not only through education but through better health. Babies born in the poorer countries will on the average have lives which are about 16 years shorter than those born in the rich countries. What are the major factors which explain the poor health record of the LDCs?

Three factors seem to be the major health determinants. First, people with lower incomes do not have the resources to buy the necessary food, housing, fuel, soap, medical services, or even water. Second, resources for public health services to provide adequate sanitation and immunization against communicable diseases may not be available. Third, the people may not have adequate education in nutrition, health, and hygiene.

One of the major reasons for the lower total life expectancy in the low-income countries is the high death rates in the first five years of life. In the rich countries only about 1 percent of children die before their fifth birthday. In contrast the figure is about 19 percent in LDCs generally and more than 40 percent in some of the world's poorest countries. In Brazil 48 percent of deaths for all causes were among children under five years of age. The contrasting figure in Sweden was only 1 percent.

The main specific causes of child deaths in LDCs are respiratory infections (especially influenza and pneumonia) and diarrheal diseases. Some diseases which have been virtually eliminated in the rich countries (e.g., measles, polio, and diphtheria) still kill millions of children in LDCs. These diseases can be prevented by vaccination, but it is estimated that less than 10 percent of the children in poor countries actually receive this care. Furthermore, malnutrition often makes the children more susceptible to disease and less able to cope with it when it strikes.

One of the most insidious ways some business interests in rich countries have contributed to high infant death rates in LDCs is through the promotion and sale of prepared formulas for feeding infants. It is generally agreed by medical experts that mother's milk is the best food for infants. It offers a balanced diet and the infant absorbs immunities from the mother. Even the best of infant food formulas require careful sterilization of bottles and of the water which is the solvent for the formula. Often sterilization is neglected not because of ignorance but because to do so would constitute another demand on already short fuel supplies.

Producers of infant food formulas have used slick promotional efforts to convince mothers to abandon traditional breast feeding in favor of bottle feeding. Advertising posters of nurses dressed in spotless white uniforms are displayed showing the nurses feeding infants with bottled formula.

"The onslaught," says Dr. Michael Latham of Cornell University, "is terrific, the message is powerful, the profits to be made are high, and high also is the resultant human suffering." Dr. Derrick Jellife, Director of the Division of Population, Family and International Health at UCLA, estimated that ten million infants each year suffered malnutrition, diarrhea, dehydration, and often death or permanent brain damage as a result of the use of bottle feeding in areas where lack of knowledge of sterilization and the lack of clean water made the safe use of infant food formula difficult. I understand that the Nestlé company, often the object of foreign criticism for its advertising methods in promoting the sale of infant food formula, has now discontinued its promotional efforts along these lines.

Accidental death rates are unusually high in the poorer countries. Deaths per vehicle mile are 16 times higher in Nigeria than in the United States. This is partly caused by inexperienced or reckless operators who drive too fast for the condition of the roads. Poorer countries do not have the financial resources to construct four-lane highways and overpasses which reduce the accident rate per-vehicle mile. Instead, motor vehicles share the roads with bicycles, pedestrians, and animals. Accident rates in factories tend to be higher because of lower standards of job safety.

Health facilities are being constructed throughout the poorer countries. The health budget of the country may be augmented by grants received from churches, foundations, and governments of other countries. But often the greatest impact is made, not by the modern and well-equipped hospital in the cities, but by small clinics which have been built in rural areas. Even if the clinics are staffed only by paramedics, inoculations can be given, antibiotics can be administered, and demonstrations of better health practices can be conducted. One of the functions of hospitals in urban areas is to give training to paramedics who will serve in rural areas. China's health clinics are a positive example of effective use of paramedical personnel.

Sanitary facilities need to be improved in many LDCs. Open sewers in urban centers cause the spread of many debilitating diseases. Sanitary toilet facilities are usually lacking in rural areas and often even in urban areas as well. Intestinal parasites flourish under such conditions and damage the health of millions of people, especially since many of these people lack the money (and sometimes the inclination) to wear shoes.

Better health would contribute much to the improvement of

human capital. Priorities must be directed toward the expenditures required for this. Until this has been accomplished, economic development will be retarded.

Questions for further study and discussion

1. What are some of the noneconomic benefits of primary education? Why are parents in LDCs often reluctant to permit their children to attend school?

2. Equal educational opportunity for boys and girls can be defended on the grounds of the inherent equal worth of all human beings. But more boys than girls are sent to schools in LDCs. Why? What are some of the special benefits which the education of girls can contribute to the development of a country?

3. What special contributions can expatriate personnel make to the staffing of secondary schools in LDCs? What are some of their limitations?

4. How can international student programs in colleges and universities in rich countries contribute to the development of LDCs? What are some of the limitations of such programs?

5. What are the costs to LDCs of the brain drain? Are these costs balanced by a compensating gain in the recipient country? What should be the attitude of recipient countries toward the brain drain from the LDCs?

6. Is it possible that an LDC may be spending too large a share of its GNP for education? What, if any, are the signs that this may in fact be happening?

7. What do you consider to be the most important ways the richer nations can contribute to the health of people in LDCs?

8. Is infant food formula a suitable way to provide nourishment for babies in LDCs? What steps, if any, should be taken to restrict the sale by multinational firms of infant food formulas to mothers in LDCs?

6

Stimulating Industrial Development

I have already pointed out that the poor countries of the world are primarily agricultural. The great majority of the people are engaged in subsistence farming—producing food for the needs of their families. To be sure, subsistence agriculture is accompanied by the production of simple houses and furniture for family use, some clothing and often primitive tools. But this small-scale manufacturing is hardly the basis for an industrial society. LDCs feel the need of industrial development as a major means of achieving the more affluent life to which they aspire.

Agriculture, though still an important feature of the total output of the rich countries (indeed, some rich countries produce burdensome surpluses of agricultural products), has long since been outstripped by the production of manufactured goods. Superficially, it would seem reasonable that if the poor countries wish to develop, they should industrialize. This chapter will examine ways in which industrial production may be stimulated in the LDCs and the relationship of industrial development to overall economic development.

The experience of the socialist countries (such as the Soviet Union) has caused some LDCs to look with interest toward the use of a rigid socialism or state capitalism to achieve industrialization. Much of the economic history of the Soviet Union in the past 65 years has been one of forced industrialization. Farmers have been greatly hurt by many of the policies which have been followed. Indeed, many of the most prosperous of the prerevolutionary farmers were either ruthlessly liquidated or they migrated to other parts of the world—especially to North America. But in spite of the enormous human costs which these policies have entailed, Russia has grown into an industrial giant. Leaders of LDCs have, of course, been quick to recognize these facts.

During the past 25 years, some of the previously poor countries have developed into what we call NICs (newly industrialized countries). Examples of these include South Korea, Taiwan, and Singapore in East Asia and Brazil and Mexico in the Western Hemisphere. These countries now are not only supplying their own needs for many manufactured products which were previously imported from abroad; they have also aggressively entered the world export market in products such as textiles, shoes, and even steel, metal products, and electronic goods. The exports from these NICs have begun to threaten similar industries in the older industrial countries. Can other LDCs also "graduate" into the status of NICs? How?

The factors that make for effective manufacturing development are highly complex. What has worked well in some countries will not necessarily be successful in others. But it is generally recognized that emphasis must be placed on at least the following three items.

Agricultural Development

First, agricultural development should not be sacrificed for industrial development. Instead, complementary development of industry and agriculture is the better policy. As the agricultural base of the economy becomes more productive, this in itself will stimulate manufacturing in various ways. It should supply reasonably cheap food for industrial workers. It will provide most of the raw materials for new industries established to process the agricultural products. The export of agricultural products will supply foreign exchange required to finance the imports of machinery necessary for industrialization.

As agriculture develops, the income of the farmers increases and as a result the domestic demand for industrial products grows. Studies show that increases in the incomes of small farmers have a greater effect on the enhancement of demand for locally produced industrial products than similar increases in the incomes of the large farms. As the farmers' incomes expand, they will be able to spend some of their added income on textiles and other consumer goods. They will also buy fertilizers and agricultural implements. If these items are produced by local industries, agricultural and industrial development will go together, each stimulating the other.

Success is most likely if government policy toward agricultural development is an enlightened one. In their desire to acquire the capital to stimulate rapid industrialization, some countries have placed unreasonable taxes on agricultural exports. Or they may have imposed artificially low prices on agricultural products sold in the countries' urban areas so as to make food cheap for the industrial workers. Or they may have exacted heavy tariffs or placed other trade barriers on the imports of products bought by farmers which the government now wants to produce in newly developing domestic industries. One or more of such policies may reduce the incentive and the ability of farmers to be productive. In this way they will retard agricultural production and in the end do damage to industrial development as well.

In an effort to increase the production of manufactured goods, some of the NICs also made heavy investments in agricultural development. South Korea, Malaysia, and Taiwan are examples of this. They spent large amounts of money to improve their land through extensive irrigation projects. They engaged in agricultural research. And they developed methods of reducing the selling prices of agricultural products by improving roads and developing more adequate marketing mechanisms.

In contrast, less successful LDCs did not give sufficient attention to agricultural development. Examples of this lack occurred in such diverse countries as Jamaica, Zambia, and Chile.

As a result they have had to import food and thus use scarce foreign exchange for this purpose which might otherwise have been used for industrial development.

Education and Training

Second, education and training are essential for industrial development. The importance of education for all kinds of economic development was emphasized in chapter 5. But education is especially important for industrial development. It is estimated that 95 percent of the world's total expenditures for research and development are made by countries that are already economically developed. The results of some of this research are, of course, kept secret. But in a relatively short time much of it is available to anyone who can read. People with more highly trained skills are needed to select from the wide variety of technology available which is most readily adaptable to industrial development.

As factories are built, people are needed to operate them. Much of the education required for this work can be acquired while working at the job. But those workers who have already mastered the basic skills of at least primary education will make more rapid progress in on-the-job training and will adapt more readily to situations which are not completely routine. It is not an accident that those countries which have developed industries most rapidly have also been those which have emphasized the development of human capital by allocating substantial resources to their educational system.

Infrastructure

Third, industrial development cannot come suddenly to a primitive subsistence economy. All but the most elementary forms of local manufacturing will require the prior development of an infrastructure. Roads must be built, seaport and airport facilities must be provided and in some cases, railways as well. Utilities must be constructed to produce and distribute power and to provide the water, sewerage, and telecommunication services needed for the growth of industrial activities.

All these require a substantial amount of capital. In the

initial stages at least, the sale of these services to manufacturing establishments cannot be made at prices which will cover the total cost of producing them. This means that they must be undertaken by governments.

But should governments continue to price these services below their cost of production? This is part of a general question of public versus private ownership of industrial facilities, and I will return to this question later in this chapter. Suffice it to make the obvious point here that the longer pricing below cost is continued,the greater will be the strain on the government budget. Furthermore, pricing below cost gives misleading signals for investment decisions by private firms, causing them to venture into programs which do not have a long-range viability. In addition, it undermines the managerial and financial autonomy of the utilities themselves.

In addition to these three fundamentals of industrial development, there are at least four other decisions which countries must make as they seek to industrialize.

First, should the industries being developed aim primarily at import substitution or at production intended largely for export? A country which seeks to industrialize will have a growing need for foreign exchange. It must have foreign currencies to buy manufacturing equipment and most likely some of the raw materials as well. If it is not an oil-producing country, it will need foreign exchange to buy oil from abroad. It will also have to import some of the items for building the requisite infrastructure. Where will the money come from?

Some of it can be borrowed. Some of it can be earned by exporting agricultural products, and this is one of the reasons for emphasizing agricultural development as a concomitant of industrial development. Some of it can be earned by exporting a part of the products of their newly established manufacturing establishments.

But saving foreign exchange contributes just as effectively as earning it. If they can produce within the country products which they formerly bought from abroad, they will be saving foreign exchange. Programs to do this are what we call *import substitution.*

Labor-intensive nondurable consumer goods, such as textiles and shoes, are the most likely initial candidates for import substitution. The production of such goods is fairly simple and is also reasonably efficient even when only relatively small amounts are produced. But care must be taken not to emphasize import substitution industries at the expense of agricultural development. As noted above, a growing rural market is needed to stimulate demand for the new manufactured products.

Instead of developing import substitution industries, some LDCs have directed their industrialization programs toward producing goods for export. The experience of Brazil demonstrates the possibility of gaining foreign exchange through a substantial growth of exports of manufactured products. In 1962 Brazil exported only $62 million (in U.S. dollars) of manufactured products. By 1982 this had grown to $7,971 million. Of course a part of this growth reflected the fact that U.S. dollars were worth less in 1982 than they were 20 years earlier. But even if one adjusts the figures for changes in the value of the dollar, Brazilian-manufactured exports enjoyed a fortyfold growth in volume in only two decades.

South Korea has shown an even more amazing growth in manufactured exports. By 1983 it was exporting nearly $25 billion. Compared with 1962, this was nearly an 800-fold increase. The figures for Singapore and Hong Kong are also impressive, but they, of course, have a much smaller domestic market than Brazil or South Korea.

The available evidence makes it difficult to generalize on the relative merits of an industrialization path that stresses import substitution and one that emphasizes a growing volume of manufactured exports. However, a governmentally directed program of import substitution would appear to be more appropriate only for the early stages of industrialization. Over the long run it is not economically desirable if it requires a continuing restriction of imports. I will be looking at questions of import protectionism under my fourth point below.

Second, where shall the capital needed for industrialization come from? All capital formation is a result of saving. Even the people of a poor country will probably voluntarily save some money if they see opportunities for profitable investment. But the volume of such saving is likely to be much too small for the investment needed for industrialization. This is especially true of the capital required for large infrastructure projects. Private saving must be supplemented by governmental saving or by borrowing abroad. Governmental saving is in reality forced saving because it stems either from levying taxes or through inflation of the currency. Money which is borrowed abroad must ultimately be paid back with interest. All of these methods impose real costs on the borrower. They can be justified economically only if the investments made from these funds serve an economically significant purpose.

Some countries have created development banks to channel funds into ventures which they would like to foster. Others have relied mainly on funds borrowed from international agencies such as the World Bank or from private sources. I will discuss the debt burden of developing countries later on in this chapter.

Development banks may supply technical services to the growing industries. They may monitor the recipient industries to ascertain whether the funds are being wisely used. They may assist the domestic firms, whether public or private, in determining whether they should go forward on their own or whether they should rely on technical assistance, capital, and perhaps control by foreign transnational firms seeking to establish industries within their borders.

In the 1950s and the 1960s many development economists emphasized the importance of a massive transfer of capital from the developed nations to the developing nations. In part, this was an outgrowth of the success of Marshall Plan aid for the reconstruction of Europe. From 1948 to 1952 the United States made Marshall Plan grants to Europe in amounts equal to about 2 percent of American GNP. These grants greatly assisted the rapid reconstruction of a war-torn Europe but they did not constitute an undue drain on the American economy.

By the 1960s the United Nations launched its First Development Decade. The poorer countries of the world, speaking through UNCTAD (United Nations Conference on Trade and Development), were deeply dissatisfied with the concrete results of this decade of effort. In their sixth and seventh special sessions, the United Nations General Assembly (1974-75) passed resolutions calling for a New International Economic Order (NIEO).

The NIEO asked for a substantial increase in the flow of capital from the rich to the poorer nations. Specifically, it requested that grants of 0.7 percent of GNP be made annually by the rich countries with special emphasis on aid to the LDCs. The record of the seven major industrialized nations:

Official Development Aid as a Percent of GNP

	1979	1984
France	0.60	0.79
Canada	0.48	0.49
West Germany	0.45	0.48
Japan	0.27	0.29
United Kingdom (Britain)	0.52	0.33
Italy	0.08	0.31
United States	0.20	0.24

It is clear that of these seven nations only France ever reached the 0.7 percent goal requested by the poorer nations. In 1984 the United States had proportionally the poorest record of any of the seven nations.

There is a question of whether a shortage of capital is the most important factor leading to a poor record of economic development in general and to a lack of industrial development in particular. Many of the poorest countries have a very limited capacity to absorb additional capital. They have not yet made maximum use of previously transferred capital. They will need to develop management skills. They will need to develop small-scale projects which require management skills unique to their situation. These, rather than infusions of foreign capital, may offer the most promise.

The poor record of the United States, however, is not due to the ability of the poor nations to absorb a greater amount of aid. Rather it results from the American preoccupation with military considerations. Today much of American foreign aid is military aid. Most of this goes to a few countries which are considered to be of strategic importance to American objectives of countering the perceived Soviet military threat. Even purely economic aid is channeled in disproportionate amounts to countries thought to be of strategic importance to American foreign policy objectives.

Some governments—particularly those of countries at a low level of economic development—have intervened in industrial development and planning so much as to deter rather than promote development. Often the coordination was faulty, cost overruns were frequent, and the government planning officials were slow to make changes to adapt to unforeseen needs. These problems are not absent in highly developed economies, but they can be particularly troublesome when a poor country is just embarking on a program of industrial development.

Third, should industries in LDCs be privately owned or governmentally owned? In its broadest sense, one may be tempted to view this as a capitalism vs. communism issue. The U.S. is often considered the leader of the capitalism school; the Soviet Union is the prime communist power. But this is a superficial view of the matter. The U.S. is not "purely capitalist." In 1984 19 percent of total U.S. GNP was represented by government consumption. On the other hand, the USSR has a very sizable private sector.

In LDCs household manufacturing is, of course, largely privately owned. If manufacturing industry can evolve slowly from this beginning it may require little more than a gradual expansion of an already incipient industry. But this may be considered too slow a process. It is also completely inadequate to care for the establishment of industries which by their nature are too large to be feasible for household production. Government ownership and operation may appear to be the only genuine alternative.

In the nineteenth century, Japan embarked on an intensive program of government establishment and ownership of industrial firms. As the industries became mature, they were sold to private enterprise. Even the United States has used governmentally owned industries, especially where military considerations were involved. Crash programs for the construction of naval vessels and the creation of synthetic rubber plants in the early years of World War II are examples. These, too, were later sold to private enterprise.

In recent years, Argentina, South Korea, Brazil and Singapore have followed policies similar to that of nineteenth-century Japan. As the governments gained funds from the sale of established industries, the proceeds were used to start new ventures which when successful were also sold for private operation.

It is generally agreed that such industries as petrochemicals, steel, and fertilizer require a large amount of capital and that in most countries they must be initiated by government ownership and operation. But there are many pitfalls. The government may insist on prices for the output which are below the cost of production. This is especially true where the output (of fertilizer, e.g.) is sold to local farmers or where it becomes the major input of other developing local industries. The government may find it difficult to ·resist the pressure of workers for higher wages even though the wage level is already higher than for comparable jobs in the private sector.

The inefficiencies of government ownership and operation create problems in some cases. In contrast to private enterprise, bankruptcy (or the fear of it) does not provide the incentive for reorganization on more efficient lines. These and other factors may cause the governmentally owned industry to operate at a loss over an extended period of time. It thus may become a drain on an already burdened government budget or the losses may be financed through creation of credit by the central bank. In either case it is a burden on the economy. Furthermore, it is likely to contribute to severe inflationary pressures.

In this discussion I have assumed that government ownership implies government operation as well. But the two need not necessarily be combined. The large amounts of capital required for some industries may make government ownership the only feasible course. But even under government ownership, recent experience in China and elsewhere suggests that it is preferable to have a management firm—with an incentive contract—operate the enterprise.

Fourth, how much protection should the government grant its developing industries against the competition of well-established foreign suppliers? The "infant industry" argument for tariff protection for incipient industrialization is one of the oldest arguments for governmental protection of industry. In his "Report on Manufactures" (1791), Alexander Hamilton, first U.S. Secretary of the Treasury, asked that Congress establish infant industry protection. Congress promptly agreed.

Economists generally accept the infant industry argument for tariffs as one of the few that may have economic validity. In some lines of manufacturing, unit costs of production decline as output expands. If a small incipient industry in a developing country needs to compete with established industries abroad, it may be impossible to do so. But if the infant industry can be protected from this foreign competition until it has grown to a more efficient size, it may then be able to stand on its own feet without protection.

It is sometimes argued that the costs of some of the factors of production in an LDC are a poor indicator of their real social cost. In particular, the labor in an LDC may presently be unemployed either openly or in a disguised form. The social cost of this presently underutilized labor may be much below its market price. Getting even a small return from this labor may be more economical than getting no return at all from unemployed workers. The social costs of the unemployment should be considered carefully. Calculations based on real social costs may show that a new industry may be profitable for the economy as a whole even though it would not be attractive to a private entrepreneur.

This argument is sound. In economic terms we need to differentiate between the economic rate of return and the financial rate of return. Using otherwise unemployed resources—especially labor—may not provide an immediate financial benefit. But using presently unemployed labor is desirable when one looks at all of the broad economic implications of the policy.

With the exception of Hong Kong, all of the currently industrializing countries have given at least some protection to domestic producers. Mexico, Brazil, and Turkey have used protection to achieve favorable rates of growth for industries engaged in producing for import substitution. As the manufacturing sector grows, the industrial and entrepreneurial skills attained can be directed to other forms of industrialization as well—especially to production for export.

But it should be emphasized that infant industry protection is not a sure guarantee of successful industrialization of an economy. The justification for the infant industry argument rests on the assumption that in a reasonable period of time the industry can grow to a maturity which will enable it to operate without further protection.

But once protection is granted, it may be very difficult to remove it. The industry chosen to be protected may not be able to grow to sufficient size to stand on its own feet without protection. The local market may not now be—and because of the small population of the country may never become—large enough to enable it to achieve sufficient economies of scale. Furthermore, protection from foreign competition may cause the management of the domestic industry to become lazy and lack the incentive to innovate. The protected industry may be operated by the governing elite of the country or by their close friends and relatives who will want to enjoy the continuing benefits of "protection" rather than to pass the benefits on to the mass of the population in the form of lower prices.

The infant industry argument is more appropriate as a policy for a large country with a well-disciplined government. Unfortunately, many of the world's poorest countries are both small and poorly governed.

Third-World Debt

One of the most serious problems which prevents further industrial development of LDCs is that they are already very deeply in debt to foreign lenders. Not all of this debt was incurred for economic development in the past. When the price of oil rose so dramatically in the 1970s, those countries which did not have domestic resources of oil often needed to borrow heavily to maintain a continuing supply of this essential fuel and industrial raw material. At the same time, some of the oil-producing countries gained large surpluses of funds which were ready to be recycled through major banks in Western countries to meet the deficits of the poor countries.

This problem came to a head in the 1980s when several events occurred more or less simultaneously. In the first place, the price of oil no longer continued to rise but instead actually fell. The decline in the price of oil was accompanied by a decline in the price of many of the primary commodities which were the major exports of the indebted third-world countries. At the same time, interest rates on the foreign debts of third world countries remained very high by historical standards. The figure of critical importance is the ratio of debt service (interest payments plus contractual repayments of principal) to export earnings. In the 1970s this ratio was 12.5 percent for the low-income economies and 9.7 percent for the middle-income economies. By 1984 the ratio had grown to 13.5 and 17.2 percent, respectively.

But in the 1980s there was a shift in the borrowing policy of many of the developing countries. Instead of medium- and long-term borrowing, they were doing more short-term borrowing. Short-term loans were easier to get, but because they had to be repaid quickly, the debt service to export ratio jumped dramatically in some developing countries. It actually was over 100 percent in some years for some countries. If these debt service charges were met, there would be no money at all left for economic development or for needed imports. On the other hand, if the debt services were not met, the borrower would have been in default and their future credit standing impaired. It also would have threatened the financial stability of the banks in the lending countries.

Latin-American countries were the most heavily in debt. It is estimated that their total debt was more than $300 billion and that 40 percent of this debt was owed to American banks. The political implications of this are large. Some of the Latin-American debtor countries do not have a record of political stability. President Castro of Cuba has suggested that a portion of this debt be canceled and that a moratorium be placed on the servicing of the remaining debt. It is unlikely that the American and Western European banks which have lent the money will accept this proposal. So the problem remains.

The indebtedness of African countries is smaller than that of Latin-American countries, but their ability to service the debt is even more limited. In the early 1980s the International Monetary Fund made loans of more than $7 billion to African countries. Some of the countries, such as Sudan, are already in default on some of this borrowing, partly because drought has both curtailed their ability to export and increased their needs to import. Some economists feel that Liberia, Zambia, and Gambia may soon be in similar trouble.

It is easy for leaders of LDCs to call for forgiveness of debts. The immediate instincts of Christians also would lead to a similar conclusion. The Catholic bishops, in their pastoral letter on economics, have taken this position. All Christians need to give serious consideration to it.

But the problem is a very complex one. If large banks fail as a result of the default of third world debts, these failures would create problems for many smaller banks which are in correspondent relationships with them. Furthermore, if these are American banks, the deposits in them are guaranteed by the Federal Deposit Insurance Corporation (FDIC). Similar insurance provisions are also made in Canada and other industrial countries for deposits in their banks. Although the FDIC has current reserves of more than $19 billion, this would not be adequate to meet obligations stemming from wholesale failures of large U.S. banks. In such a situation, the U.S. federal government would need to supply the funds required for the satisfaction of the depositors' claims.

The problem is exacerbated by the fact that some of the banks which lent the money went far beyond prudent banking in making the loans in the first place. They may have been motivated to do this by the prospect of large profits from the loans.

If the U.S. government starts bailing out private banks, will it do so only for those banks which had made prudent loans? Who would decide which loans were prudent?

We need to think of creative new approaches to the problem of third-world debt. Recently a suggestion was made that in the first instance the debtor countries should not repay the first-world banks or businesses which made the loans. Instead, they should make their payments to a revolving fund. This fund should be administered by an international agency. As payments were made into the fund the creditor countries would be given stock in the fund equal to these payments. The fund itself would be used to provide new investments in the third world countries making payments into the fund.

Both the debtor and the creditor countries would have a strong interest in making the project work. The debtor countries would be protecting their credit standing and would use the resources from the fund for further development. The creditor countries would have equity capital in the fund rather than defaulted loans.

Under such a plan, the condition of the debtor countries would ultimately improve so that they could retire the foreign-owned equity capital. It is unlikely that such a scheme would work for all third-world debt. But if it were only partially successful, it would be better than a stream of defaults or a burden on the debtor countries so severe as to inhibit their further development and thus their ability to pay their debts.

The problem of third world debt thus is potentially very serious for the further industrial development of LDCs. Although the problem is a serious one for all LDCs, it is especially troublesome for the poorest of the LDCs. It could also become a serious problem for the financial stability of our major international financial institutions. But the human costs are the most serious on the very poor people of the world. A new international economic conference of both lending and borrowing countries is urgently needed. At such a conference the voices of the poorest of the LDCs must be heard and appropriate actions must be taken to respond creatively to what the poor are saying.

Questions for further study and discussion

1. How can agricultural development in an LDC serve to stimulate industrial development?

2. What types of educational programs are most likely to provide the skills which are required for industrial development?

3. What are the factors which determine whether an LDC seeking to industrialize should emphasize import substitution rather than produce manufactured products for an export market?

4. How much of the capital required for industrial development should be provided by the resources within the LDC and how much should be borrowed abroad? What are the hazards involved in accumulating too large a debt to overseas lenders? Will excessive dependence on capital derived from domestic savings unduly retard the progress of industrialization?

5. What are the advantages and problems of industrialization through government initiation and operation of the industries compared with reliance on the private sector to take this initiative?

6. How valid do you consider the "infant industry" argument for trade restriction?

7. Should a moratorium be placed on third-world debt to the wealthy nations even if this means possible failure of banks in the wealthy nations or governmental intervention to absorb at least some of the losses of the lending banks?

8. Would you be willing to be taxed to help pay for defaults by debtors in LDCs?

7

International Cooperation

Many of the LDCs are small. A small country is at a disadvantage in a world dominated by great powers. What are the ways in which LDCs can help each other in the process of development? How can the developed countries help them? Even the large LDCs also can benefit from the assistance and cooperation of the international community. Unfortunately, the record of progress toward international cooperation—though it certainly is better than it was a half century ago—still leaves much to be desired. This chapter will review some of the forms which international cooperation has taken and in particular will assess the relationship of this cooperation to the development of the poor nations.

Customs Unions

Throughout most of history, each individual nation has attempted to be completely sovereign. During the Middle Ages the sovereign body was often just a small principality. Europe took a big step forward in its economic as well as its political development when groups of these small principalities united to form nation-states. But in our time of rapid transportation and communication, the nation-state is too small to be economically efficient. The nation itself can gain by cooperating

with other nations, even though this represents a partial surrender of autonomy. International trade is a primary example
of international cooperation. Whenever a nation engages in
international trade, it is, in effect, admitting its partial dependence upon other nations.

The European Economic Community (EEC) is an outstand-
ing example of international cooperation. It began in 1952 with
the formation of the European Coal and Steel Community.
This provided for a common market for coal and steel products
for six Western European nations: France, West Germany,
Italy, the Netherlands, Belgium, and Luxembourg. Five years
later the Treaty of Rome expanded the cooperation of these
same six nations as they became a customs union. This means
that they agreed to move toward a policy of free trade between
the member nations and to a common set of tariffs for products
coming into the area from the rest of the world.

The EEC has not yet achieved complete freedom of trade,
particularly in agricultural products. However, tremendous
progress has been made toward free trade and the result has
been the development of much stronger economies for all of
the countries involved. The volume of Western European trade
has expanded enormously as artificial barriers to international
trade have been removed. In 1973 Great Britain, Ireland, and
Denmark also joined the EEC. Greece, Spain, and Portugal
were added more recently.

Much attention has been paid to the economic significance
of the formation of EEC, and it is the economic aspects of
cooperation, which are the main concern of this chapter. But it
should be noted in passing that the EEC has also had important political results. France and West Germany—two of
the key members of the EEC—have been at war with each
other many times in the past centuries. In this century they
were major antagonists in both World War I and II. Comment-
ing on the formation of the European Coal and Steel Community, Maurice Schuman of France said, "Because Europe
was not united we have had war. [Now] any war between
France and Germany becomes not only unthinkable, but in
actual fact impossible." Greater political stability in Western

Europe has also contributed much to the economic development of the area.

LDCs should study the experience of the EEC. The formation and operation of the EEC represented a significant surrender of complete national autonomy. But the member countries of EEC were enriched thereby. It has also had important political implications. Inasmuch as most LDCs are small, the potential economic and political benefits they would receive from the kind of regional integration represented by the EEC are substantial. There have been several attempts by groups of LDCs to develop regional integration. Unfortunately, all of them have had much more limited success than the EEC.

In the years 1960-67 eleven countries of Latin America formed the Latin American Free Trade Association (LAFTA). A free trade association differs from a customs union in that the latter has both free trade among member countries and common trade barriers toward the outside world. In the free trade association, on the other hand, though there is free trade between member nations, each nation is free to have its own autonomous tariff policy applied to outside countries. The main advantage of the free trade association is that it is easier to form. The disadvantage is that, inasmuch as the member countries retain more autonomy, it offers fewer potential economic benefits.

In 1960 LAFTA had only seven member countries. Its progress toward achieving its ultimate goal of free trade was slow, though fairly substantial at first. By 1967 its membership had expanded to eleven countries. But these countries were spread geographically from Mexico in the north to Argentina in the south. The distances which separated them and the lack of a well-developed road and rail network between them inhibited genuine regional integration. Two years later the six members of LAFTA in the region of the Andes Mountains formed the Andean Common Market. However, Chile withdrew in 1976 and the ultimate goal of a fully functioning free trade association has still not been realized.

The Central American Common Market (CACM), consisting of five Central American countries (Costa Rica, El

Salvador, Guatemala, Honduras, and Nicaragua) was formed in 1961. Although progress was initially made toward the realization of a common market, in recent years political hostilities and mutual suspicions among the member countries have endangered its further usefulness. For example, in 1969 the "soccer war" damaged relationships between El Salvador and Honduras. More recently relationships between Honduras and Nicaragua have been strained.

There have been other attempts at economic integration among the smaller countries of the Western Hemisphere. The Caribbean Free Trade Association (CARIFTA), consisting primarily of former British colonies, was formed in 1968. The Caribbean Common Market (CARICOM) was formed in 1976. In each case relatively little progress was made toward the achievement of their goals.

Countries on other continents have also attempted to form free trade areas or common markets. The East African Economic Community was a common market formed in 1967 and consisted of Kenya, Uganda, and Tanzania. On the surface this would appear to be an ideal association of countries on a regional basis. They have common frontiers and, as former parts of the British Empire, they shared in British development efforts. But the association broke up in 1977 because of hostilities between the member countries. These hostilities still divide them.

The Association of South East Asian Nations (ASEAN) was formed in 1975 and was designed to be a free trade area consisting of Indonesia, Malaysia, the Philippines, Singapore, and Thailand. Brunei was added to the group in 1984. By 1986 the ASEAN group had made relatively little progress toward achieving free trade within the member countries. Tariff reductions have been made on products which accounted for less than 5 percent of intra-ASEAN trade. For example, the Philippines reduced from 20 to 18 percent its tariff on snow plows imported from other ASEAN countries!

The formation of regional economic blocs of small LDCs is in part the result of a desire to form a united front in dealing with the larger economies of North America and Europe. But they must face the realities that they are often composed of competitive rather than complementary economies. Historically, many of these countries have traded relatively little between themselves. Their transportation facilities have been built for trade with Europe and North America rather than for trade with each other. This makes a strong union much more difficult than it was for the EEC.

In Western Europe the formation of the EEC gave still further impetus to a mutual trade which was already well developed. In 1984, 53 percent of exports from countries within the EEC went to other members of the EEC. This contrasts with only 17 percent for members of ASEAN. Most of the intra-ASEAN trade was with a single member of the group—Singapore.

The experiences of EEC—difficult though they have been at times—should stimulate the smaller LDCs of the world to continue to strive toward the goal of greater economic unity and mutual interdependence. It is one of the ironies of our time that already wealthy nations become still more affluent through regional integration. On the other hand, poor nations which so desperately need to raise their standard of living have so often demonstrated their inability to develop effective cooperation.

Small economies are not necessarily poor. Some small countries (e.g., Hong Kong) have made very substantial economic progress. But where small size is accompanied by political hostility toward neighbors, the prognosis is poor.

International Commodity Agreements

In chapter 2 I noted that one of the characteristics of the smaller LDCs is their dependence on the export of only one or two products. Both the supply and demand of these products often fluctuate widely from one year to another. This leads to erratic fluctuations in the prices of the products and consequently in the income of the LDCs. It is a problem similar to that faced by farmers even in wealthy countries like the United States and Canada. The governments of these latter nations respond to the problem by legislation which provides price supports. Can there be effective international price supports?

An international commodity agreement is designed to stabilize the price of a primary product covered by the agreement. Ideally, the agreements should involve both consuming and producing countries. Typical examples of commodities covered by agreements are cocoa, coffee, rubber, wheat, and tin. The tin agreement involved the establishment of a buffer stock which would expand when world prices were low and would be drawn upon when prices were high. Other agreements involved production controls, export controls, and commitments to maintain a given volume of exports or imports.

Unfortunately, the experience with international commodity agreements has not been a satisfactory one. Some 40 such agreements covering 13 commodities have been signed since 1931, but their median life has been only two-and-one-half years. By 1986 only four of these agreements were still in operation. Only one of them had any influence on prices. Certainly this means that they have not realized their objectives. When commodity prices are high, the producing countries are often not interested in participating. On the other hand, during periods of depressed prices the consuming countries are not interested.

An international commodity agreement will be successful only if the great majority of producing and consuming countries participate. Most agreements have fallen short of this goal. Great Britain—formerly a major importer of wheat—did not participate in the first three of the international wheat agreements. The Soviet Union was not a part of the first four of the wheat agreements. Brazil—a major producer of sugar—was not a signatory of the first international sugar agreement. The U.S.—the world's largest importer of tin—did not participate in the first two of the international tin agreements.

Inasmuch as the agreements seek to stabilize prices, it is obvious that the price target must be carefully chosen. Neither unduly high nor unduly low prices are tenable. Attempts to conclude a cocoa agreement repeatedly failed because of a lack of agreement on price. It is best to operate on the assumption that complete price stability is impossible. Rather, the aim should be to achieve a range of prices within which supply and demand can reasonably be expected to be in equilibrium.

The International Tin Agreement called for the creation of buffer stocks of tin to promote price stability. Buffer stock arrangements have the advantage of not requiring production restrictions. But to be effective, the buffer stock needs to be sufficiently large. This was not true in the case of the tin agreements. Large buffer stocks tie up a lot of capital in inventory. The member countries were not willing to bear the costs which this would involve.

Buffer stock arrangements are not suitable for many of the other primary commodities. Some commodities are perishable if stored for an appreciable length of time and consequently do not lend themselves to buffer stock schemes. Storage costs are high relative to market price for some products.

International commodity agreements, therefore, have had only a very limited usefulness, desirable though they may appear to be from a theoretical viewpoint. Another problem is that many primary products are produced both in LDCs and in developed countries. In fact, about two-thirds of the exports of LDCs compete directly with production in developed countries. Examples of such products are oil, sugar, and cotton. For these products, the sales by LDCs are influenced largely by the national policies pursued by these large developed countries— especially by the prices at which they choose to dispose their surpluses.

If satisfactory industrial substitutes can be produced the opportunity for significant price increases for natural products from LDCs is slight. Examples of this include synthetic rubber for the natural product and synthetic textiles for wool or silk.

International commodity agreements will probably be most successful for commodities which are produced only in LDCs and for which practically no substitutes are available. Coffee, tin, cocoa, and tea are examples of such products. The demand for these products tends to be inelastic. In other words, total sales are not substantially increased when prices decline. For such products it would be more feasible to use an export tariff to raise the world price and thus to increase LDC income. Even here, however, the major producing countries would need to apply similar tariffs so that the relative position of each producing country would be the same after the tariff as it had been before. An agreement to impose similar tariffs is, of course, also a matter which would require international cooperation.

Even when international commodity agreements do not continue to function in the way that was originally planned, international councils (e.g., International Sugar Council and International Tin Council) still meet on a regular basis in some cases. This provides a medium for sharing information. The councils may also persist in their efforts to promote price stability through the negotiation of new commodity agreements.

Preferences for the Exports of LDCs

Rich countries have the resources to import products from the poor. Should they not grant special preferences to such imports so as to expand this trade and thus encourage the development of the poor countries? At the first session of UNCTAD (United Nations Conference on Trade and Development) the LDCs asked the industrial countries to give preferences to the importation of manufactured products from LDCs. The LDCs had been discouraged by the many problems they had encountered in the exportation of primary products. They viewed preferences for manufactures as an important road to development because it would stimulate industrial development.

In 1970 eighteen industrial nations agreed to establish a system of preferences for exports from LDCs. It was called a "generalized system of preferences" (GSP) because it was intended that all developed countries would participate in the program. The United States joined this group in 1976 after authorization to do so was granted by the Trade Act of 1974. From time to time since then, products have been added to or subtracted from the list of products on which preferences apply. Currently about 3000 items from 140 countries are covered. The total value of U.S. imports from countries to which U.S. GSP applies was $88 billion in 1983. Of these imports, only one-fourth were eligible for GSP treatment and less than one-eighth were granted duty-free import status. The total value of imports enjoying this preferred position was only 4.2 percent of U.S. imports from all sources in 1983. Though a relatively small part of total U.S. foreign trade, these imports were crucial to the economic development of certain LDCs.

GSP was a partial response to the slogan "trade, not aid." In 1984, the LDCs who were not oil exporters earned a total of $254 billion in exports. In addition the oil exporting LDCs earned $268 billion in exports. In the same year, official development assistance was only $38 billion. Trade was more than 11 times as important as aid to LDCs.

The rich countries should be encouraged to enhance the trade of LDCs by being more generous in their application of GSP. The political problems of doing so, however, are formidable. Textiles, leather products, petroleum products, and steel are not included in the GSP of any of the industrial nations. Such products are often labor intensive. They are thus particularly well adapted to efficient production in LDCs where labor costs are low. But there are also substantial pressure groups of persons employed in these industries in the rich countries who are afraid that they will lose their jobs as a result of imports. If, in fact, employment declines for whatever reason, they exert political pressure to restrict imports.

On the other hand, consumers who pay lower prices for the imported products because of tariff preferences are usually not organized. Most do not realize that they have benefited from the GSP. This is especially unfortunate since the consumers in developed countries who benefit most by lower tariffs on imports are often the poor who may be able to afford only the inexpensive imported product.

GSP is not likely to be of much help to the poorest of the LDCs. More than 80 percent of the imports covered by GSP came from only ten of the 140 countries to which the U.S. has extended GSP. Taiwan, Korea, and Hong Kong accounted for over half of the duty-free imports under this program. These countries would probably have developed even in the absence of GSP.

In conclusion, GSP is significant. It should be encouraged. It should be expanded in the scope of products covered and extended to other countries.

But we must look to other ways to meet the problems of the world's poorest countries.

International Lending Agencies

Nations cooperate with each other by borrowing and lending money. Although we call these loans "international," most of them are made privately by banks and by businesses which seek to extend their operations abroad. However, since the end of World War II, a number of international agencies have been placed in operation. Though the total volume of lending by these agencies is still not nearly as large as private lending, they are growing in importance. Their work needs to be expanded so that they may more adequately meet the needs of LDCs. In the paragraphs which follow some of the most important ones will be described.

In July 1944, during the closing months of World War II, 44 nations met at a resort hotel in Bretton Woods, New Hampshire, to lay plans for international monetary cooperation in the postwar period. The economic chaos of the 1930s which stemmed in part from misguided economic policies following World War I underscored the need for cooperation after World War II. It was hoped that the economic mistakes of the post-World War I period would not be repeated.

During much of the nineteenth century and the early years of the twentieth century, the international gold standard dominated the international monetary scene. It was quickly abandoned by most nations during World War I. By the mid-1920s, it was reestablished, but it could not survive the stresses caused by the Great Depression in the 1930s.

However, representatives at the Bretton Woods Conference decided that as soon as possible after the conclusion of World War II, two new international lending agencies should be established: the International Bank for Reconstruction and Development (IBRD) and the International Monetary Fund (IMF).

World Bank

The IBRD (popularly called the World Bank) was designed to make long-term loans to its member countries. During the first five years these loans were made primarily to reconstruct the war-torn economies of Europe. But since then the main focus has shifted from reconstruction to development. By 1985 over $80 billion in loans had been made. Most of the development loans have been made on a long-term basis (up to 35 years) for such projects as road building, hydroelectric power, port facilities, and irrigation works.

Each country which joins the World Bank must make an initial contribution of capital in proportion to its economic resources. However, this has been augmented by funds which the World Bank receives by selling its bonds on world financial markets. The loans are made in hard currency (usually in U.S. dollars) and they must be repaid with interest at market rates in similar currency.

The stringent repayment provisions of the IBRD make it difficult for the world's poorest countries to qualify for a loan. This led to the establishment in 1961 of the International Development Association (IDA). Often referred to as the "soft loan" window of the World Bank, IDA makes loans with maturities of up to 50 years to developing countries. After a grace period of ten years these loans are scheduled for repayment without interest, except a modest service charge. Unlike IBRD, IDA does not have its own capital. Instead, it is dependent on money contributed by the richer countries through their international aid programs.

Unfortunately, the American contribution to IDA has been cut. Budget deficits resulting from reduced tax rates and increased military spending have led to cuts in many of the nonmilitary aspects of the U.S. federal budget. In 1984 the American commitment to IDA was reduced by $195 million a year for a three-year period. This was a distressing response to IDA's request for an increase of $55 million a year. Other nations usually match the American contribution on a 3-to-1 basis. Therefore, the American cutback was a severe blow to the future work of IDA. A. W. Clausen, then president of the

World Bank, said that the cut condemned millions to abject poverty and may contribute to political instability in the countries which were counting on the aid.

IDA has now lent about $30 billion. Poor countries with large populations such as India, Bangladesh, and Pakistan have received substantial sums from IDA. Its loans have been highly important in meeting crucial needs of some of the world's poorest countries.

The International Finance Corporation (IFC) was established in 1956 as another subsidiary of the World Bank. It does not make loans to governments; rather, it participates along with private investors in business projects. Sometimes it lends the money. Sometimes it becomes a part owner. The total volume of its loans has been only about $4 billion. Thus, it is by a wide margin the smallest of the three agencies which comprise the "World Bank Group." However, in 1985 the United States and other major Western countries agreed to double the capital of the IFC to $1.3 billion. When this money is contributed, the IFC will be able to commit up to $7.3 billion for 400 new investments with a total value of about $30 billion.

There are also other international lending agencies not connected with the World Bank but which operate on principles somewhat similar to those of the World Bank. The largest of these is the Inter-American Development Bank. It was started through the cooperation of the United States with all of the Latin-American countries except Cuba. Like the IBRD, it has its "hard-currency window," where it makes loans at market rates and a "soft-currency window" where it utilizes special funds for loans on easy terms. It also has a Social Program Trust Fund to finance education, low-income housing, and other social projects. Its loans have totaled about $20 billion.

Some development banks operate on a regional basis. The Asian Development Bank was organized in 1966 by 19 Asian countries with the cooperation of 11 European countries, Canada, and the United States. It has made loans of about $10 billion. The African Development Bank was started in 1964 with a membership limited to the independent countries of Africa. Its loans thus far have been less than $2 billion.

The United Nations has also sponsored its own development program (UNDP) and other agencies such as its children's fund (UNICEF). These agencies have made grants totaling about $7 billion. They have made almost no loans.

The total amount of help these various international agencies have given has been far less than that requested by the LDCs. They have called for a massive transfer of resources from the first to the third world through a New International Economic Order (NIEO). But the international agencies established thus far represent an important beginning. They should be more adequately financed in the future.

International Monetary Fund

The International Monetary Fund (IMF) is the second major agency established by the Bretton Woods Conference. Unlike the World Bank group, the IMF was originally designed to make only short-term loans for the purpose of stabilizing foreign-exchange rates. Each member country announced its proposed exchange rate with the U.S. dollar. Inasmuch as the dollar was assumed to have a fixed relationship with gold, in effect an international gold-exchange standard was thus established. If subsequent events showed that the initial exchange rate was not a viable one, it would be "adjusted." Short-term pressures on exchange rates, however, could be cared for by borrowing from or lending to the IMF.

The resources of the IMF came from contributions of its members as they fulfilled their "quotas." The size of these quotas was determined by such things as the GNP of the countries, their volume of foreign trade, and the adequacy of their gold reserves. At the close of World War II, the United States was in a much stronger position in all of these ways than any other country. Therefore, initially the U.S. contributed 34.2 percent of the total $8 billion resources of the IMF. Great Britain had the second largest quota. Together the two Anglo-Saxon countries contributed over half of the total resources of the IMF. Three-fourths of the quota contributions were made in the currency of the contributing country. The other one-fourth consisted of gold.

In 1971 the United States by unilateral action severed the connection between the dollar and gold. Although there was an attempt later that year to establish a new gold-dollar parity, by 1973 this, too, had been abandoned.

But the IMF now turned to a number of new activities. In particular it moved from giving exclusive attention to short-term loans to providing an "extended facility" which made loans for longer periods and in larger amounts. In the early years, IMF loans seldom totaled more than $2 billion a year. This figure expanded considerably in the late 1970s and still more in the 1980s. Total loans in 1984 were about $32 billion.

Many of the larger loans were made to the LDCs. Some of these loans were granted to compensate for the low prices these countries were getting for their exports of primary products. Some were made to meet the demands stemming from high prices LDCs had to pay for imports of oil and manufactured goods. Some, unfortunately, were made because the countries had embarked on expensive programs of expanding their military forces and buying sophisticated military hardware. The total volume of LDC indebtedness is so high relative to the resources of the IMF that some have expressed fear for its continued financial stability. A default on any of these loans would, of course, severely damage the credit rating of the defaulting country with the IMF. But it could also lead to an ugly situation in international relations.

Two steps have been taken to cope with these problems. The one is a series of increases in the quotas of member countries. The other, of lesser immediate but perhaps much more long term significance, is the authorization of the IMF to issue its own international money called Special Drawing Rights. These two steps will now be described in turn.

When the IMF began operation in 1946, the total of the quotas was only $8 billion. These quotas have been increased a number of times since then, most recently in 1984. The total now is approximately $80 billion. The number of countries participating has grown to 147. Practically all of the noncommunist countries of the world (except Switzerland) are now members. In the communist group Romania, Hungary, Yugoslavia, the People's Republic of China, and others have joined. Each new country added has brought with it its own quota of contributions to the resources of the IMF. Quotas of the original members were also increased. However, other countries' quotas have expanded more than the U.S. quota. The result is that the U.S. share has now been reduced from the original 34.2 percent to its present 20.1 percent.

Voting power in decisions of the IMF is proportional to the quotas held. This means that the U.S. still wields much power and influence. In the eyes of some leaders in LDCs, both the World Bank and the IMF are American-dominated institutions.

Many of the recent IMF loans were made to LDCs which are in financial difficulty. The International Monetary-Fund management has made such loans with the stipulation that the recipient country engage in national economic policies of "austerity." This means that they must balance their national budgets and pursue restrictive monetary and fiscal policies. The measures used fall most heavily on the working classes and the poor. The policies usually require higher taxes and lower wages. Sometimes massive layoffs and higher unemployment have resulted. Cuts in vital services and reduced governmental food subsidies have led to demonstrations of protest in Brazil, the Dominican Republic, Morocco, Poland, and Tunisia.

The "IMF riots," a term coined by the press in some of these countries, express a popular hostility to IMF policies. Much of this hostility is directed against the United States. The LDCs ask why they must balance their budgets when the United States accumulates record budget deficits. French writers have accused the U.S. of having "deficits without tears." IMF advice for budget-balancing could be taken by the LDCs with greater grace if they were not also aware that the dominant power making the stipulation has its own financial difficulties and is hardly meeting them with austerity. Largely because of its recent military buildup, the budget deficit of the U.S. is now the largest of any country in the world. But it has taken only inadequate steps to increase taxes or reduce expenditures to meet it.

The international money issued by the IMF (Special Drawing Rights, SDR) has also appeared to the LDCs to have been "stacked" to favor the rich countries. The question of whether they should be issued at all goes back to one of the fundamental differences of opinion evident at the Bretton Woods Conference in 1944. There the British delegation, led by economist John Maynard (Lord) Keynes, argued that the Fund should assume more the form of a bank. It would be an international central bank patterned after the national central banks already existing in practically every country. The Federal Reserve Banks are the central banks of the U.S. and they now issue all of the paper money used in this country. Similarly, the paper money of most of the countries of the world consists entirely of their own central bank notes. Keynes argued that the new international bank should likewise be qualified to issue a paper money. He suggested that it be called "bancor," implying that it be a paper gold issued by a bank.

The American delegation to the Bretton Woods Conference objected to this suggestion and it was dropped from the plan which was finally approved. Less than 20 years after the Bretton Woods Conference, however, officials from the U.S. Treasury realized that their position was wrong and argued instead that the IMF be authorized to issue its own paper money. This was approved in 1969 and in the three years following, over $9 billion of SDRs were issued. Again in 1979 another issue was authorized over a three-year period. The total SDRs now outstanding is about $22 billion. Of this total, the U.S. currently holds over $8 billion, more than one-third of the total.

Why has the U.S. received such a large share of the SDRs issued? Because they have been distributed in proportion to the quotas of the member nations. This arrangement has been severely criticized—not only by the representatives from the LDCs but by many thoughtful people in the developed countries as well. Sir Dudley Stamp of England has recommended a "link" arrangement. His plan calls for the issue of SDRs not according to national quotas of contributions to the Fund, but in relation to the needs of the poorer nations for development.

The charter of the IMF presently requires an 85 percent vote on matters pertaining to SDRs. Until this is changed there is scant possibility that anything like the link proposal will be adopted. Leaders from rich nations fear that it would result in an excessive issue of paper money and that this would contribute to worldwide inflation.

At the IMF meeting in Kingston, Jamaica, in 1976 a modest step was taken to redress the LDCs' grievance. This provided that one-sixth of the gold held by the IMF should be placed in a special trust fund and then sold for the benefit of developing countries. Thus, approximately 25 million ounces of gold became available for sale. The official price of gold since 1973 has been only $42.22 per ounce. The IMF sales, however, have been made on the open market at current market prices. The sales were made in small amounts over a period of years so that the market was not unduly affected. Market prices of gold have fluctuated greatly in recent years but they have often been 8 to 10 times the official price and at times much more than that. The profit made on the sale of this gold is to benefit LDCs (defined for this purpose as countries with a per capita GNP of less than $300).

Conclusion

I have been critical of much of the international cooperation of the past 40 years. It still is a long way from meeting the demands of the world we live in with its vast gulf between the incomes of the poor and the rich nations. But on the other hand, it represents a substantial improvement over the nearly complete lack of cooperation which characterized earlier periods of history. I feel that it is still much "too little," but we can also be stimulated to further action to make sure that it is expanded in the future before it is "too late."

Questions for further study and discussion

1. Why have customs unions between LDCs been less successful than the European Economic Community?

2. Have the difficulties experienced by LDCs in forming customs unions or free trade associations been caused by the

hostility or apathy of the rich nations? Or does the responsibility rest primarily with the leadership of the LDCs themselves? What problems presently faced by LDCs in forming customs unions were not experienced by western European countries?

3. Do you feel that the United States and Canada should seek to form a common market between themselves? Should Latin-American nations and Japan also be included in such a common market?

4. Why have international commodity agreements had such little success in stabilizing the price of primary products? Has the major focus of the difficulty been the wealthy nations which consume the products or the LDCs which produce them?

5. How can both the rich nations and the poor nations benefit from special tariff and other trade preferences for the exports of the poor nations?

6. What changes could be made in the IBRD and the IMF so that they would not be so widely regarded as American-dominated institutions? If the rich countries do not dominate these lending agencies will they continue adequately to contribute financially to them?

7. Should LDC indebtedness to American banks be forgiven (in whole or in part) even though this would result in an increase in U.S. government expenditures and taxes?

8. Should the IMF link the future issues of Special Drawing Rights to the development needs of LDCs even if this would increase the danger of world inflationary pressures?

8

What Can I Do?

Throughout this book I have emphasized the sharp differences in wealth and income between the rich and the poor nations of the world. Faced with what I hope is a heightened awareness of the seriousness of these disparities the sensitive Christian conscience may be overwhelmed with intense feelings of guilt. We certainly can't sit comfortably on the sidelines. Nor can we simply isolate ourselves from the problems. But, on the other hand, feverishly wringing our hands will not help the situation. We must do something. But what?

Emergency Food Aid

Part of our response must inevitably be a short-term reaction to an immediately demanding situation. When we see pictures of hundreds of starving people on our TV screens we want to share some of our food with them. This is a natural and desirable reaction. As we contribute to emergency food needs, we can only hope that we are not doing too little too late. And we must remember that starvation is not just a massive "problem"; it has a human face. All persons, rich and poor, are equally precious in God's eyes.

But it is also important to realize that meeting a crisis need is only a short-range approach to a complex problem. Bringing food to a country from abroad will multiply the supply of food, depressing the price of food produced locally. This is, of course, its immediate objective. But as we take this emergency step, we must recognize that our gift will make it more difficult for local farmers to produce profitably the food which must supply the long-term needs. The development problem consists in part of making it more easily possible for farmers in LDCs to expand their food production. Anything which works against this is self-defeating.

Eating Less

Another natural response by people in the rich countries who are sensitive to the needs of the poor is to say that we should eat less so that people in poor countries can have at least a little. Some people prefer to eat less meat or to eat no meat at all. In 1983 the average American consumed 1,725 pounds of grain. The average grain consumption in poor countries was 400 pounds. Americans had consumed much grain indirectly through eating meat and dairy products. People in LDCs can't afford such a rich diet.

Students on college campuses sometimes decide to fast for a day and to ask that the food service of the college use the money saved thereby as a grant to an international relief agency. This has an important symbolic significance and is praiseworthy. Jesus often talked of fasting when he spoke of prayer. The Christian will be spiritually enriched by a frequent practice of both.

Inasmuch as most people in the rich countries tend to overeat, their physical health will be enhanced by eating less. To give up food that those in poor countries may be fed, thus serves a double purpose. But such self-denial must be accompanied by an organized plan of assuring that the food we save will actually get to the world's poor.

This raises a more fundamental question. Can a reduction in the standard of living in rich countries be a means of raising the standards of living in the poor? If the resources of the world were a fixed quantity, such a program would be desirable. But the resources of the world are not—at least at this stage of history—fixed. Even nonrenewable resources such as fossil fuels are apparently much more abundant than was thought in the 1970s. It is important that production in both the rich and the poor nations be encouraged. Rich nations will thus be in a better position to give genuine help to the poor—"a better position" to do so, but whether or not it will actually be done must be a prime concern of the Christian conscience.

Boycotts

Another suggestion which is often made is that Christians in rich countries refrain from consuming certain third-world products. Some examples are bananas, carnations, and beef for our hamburgers. Such products from LDCs are often produced by multinational firms. Much of the profit from their production goes to the multinational firm whose world headquarters may be located in Europe or the United States. Furthermore, they may be produced on prime farmland which should be used to produce food for the poor of the country.

Such boycotts have a symbolic significance, and symbolism is important in itself. But unless they are accompanied by significant changes in national political policy, their impact will be minimal. They may, in fact, create hardships for people in LDCs who are now engaged in the production of these products.

Political Changes

We will now consider some of the political changes necessary for the betterment of global economics. In chapter 2 we pointed out that the governments of many LDCs are military dictatorships or single-party civilian governments where the ruling class is a wealthy elite. Such governments have the support of only a small fraction of the people of the country. Leaders arise from time to time who through revolutionary means seek to wrest control of the government. Often these leaders have been influenced by Marxist philosophy. In many cases they tend to be anti-American because they view the United States as a barrier to the political and economic reforms which they think are long overdue.

The Cold War

One of the key objectives in American foreign policy since the end of World War II has been to win the cold war with the Soviet Union. The cold war was not started by the Soviet Union alone, nor was it started by the United States alone. Like most disputes it had multiple causes. It will not serve a useful purpose here to try to assess which country or countries were the most responsible.

The conflict between the United States and the Soviet Union has had profound results, not only in these two countries, but throughout the world. When North and South Korea were at war in the early 1950s, the United States, under the umbrella of the United Nations, entered the conflict. When a revolutionary China sent troops across the Yalu River to drive American forces back to the 38th parallel, it was easy to assume that the Soviet Union and China were eager allies in a powerful attempt to make sure that communism would rule all of Asia. The Vietnam War was fought in large part because of the fear that if the North Vietnamese won, it would be only one more factor in a domino effect that would cause all of East Asia to turn communist.

Russian dominance of the Eastern European Warsaw Pact countries and evidence of Soviet atrocities such as the Katyn forest massacre provided much support for the feeling that Russia was, indeed, an "evil empire." Those who have compared life in East Germany with West Germany and have noted the Berlin wall which separates the two, find ready justification for making invidious comparisons between the communist world and the "free" world. When revolutionary movements in any of the third world countries were supported by Marxist rhetoric, it did not seem unreasonable to assume that they were a part of a grand Soviet design to rule the world. When the choice for American policymakers was a choice between a right-wing dictatorship or a left-wing revolutionary movement, the choice was almost invariably the right wing. Even though by no stretch of the imagination could these right-wing governments be called "democratic," to influential Americans they seemed to be the lesser of two evils.

Military Aid

Increasingly, American foreign aid was directed toward those trouble spots where communism seemed to be a threat. And increasingly, the foreign aid became less and less economic in nature and more and more military. There seems to be much American governmental money to support anti-communist governments, and little to support long-range economic development programs which would serve to create an environment where communism would no longer be an attractive policy alternative for the future.

Maximum progress toward meeting the needs of the poor countries cannot be made unless there is a fundamental shift in American foreign policy. For the past several decades U.S. foreign policy has been dominated by a fear of the spread of communism. Arresting this spread by whatever means seems to be required. And it has been deemed more important than improving the economies of third world countries so that communism is for them a less attractive alternative.

Christian Altruism

The means used inevitably affect the results achieved. A foreign policy which would genuinely be concerned about the welfare of the poor nations rather than the fear of what their form of economic system may do to the United States is urgently required. Nothing less than Christian altruism must replace America's currently perceived self-interest.

I realize that a government is not likely to be dominated by Christian altruism. Governments inevitably operate in terms of what they deem to be national self-interest. For this reason, the approach of the Brandt Commission may be more feasible politically.

The Brandt Commission Report

The Brandt Commission consisted of an independent group of 20 diplomats from five continents. Chaired by former West German Chancellor Willy Brandt, its report emphasized that the interests of the rich and the poor nations were mutual interests. Their very interdependence creates the possibility of reciprocal benefit. Even though this is a lesser good than freely given Christian love, it is superior to the narrow nationalism which seems to be the only criterion by which national policy is usually formulated.

The Brandt Commission report was also critical of military expenditures:

> The world's military spending dwarfs any spending on development. Total military expenditures are approaching $450 billion a year, of which over half is spent by the Soviet Union and the United States, while annual spending on official development aid is only $20 billion. If only a fraction of the money, manpower and research presently devoted to military uses were diverted to development, the future prospects of the Third World would look entirely different.
>
> In any case there is a moral link between the vast spending on arms and the disgracefully low spending on measures to remove hunger and ill-health in the Third World. The programme of the World Health Organization to abolish malaria is short of funds; it is estimated that it will eventually cost about $450 million—which represents only about one-thousandth of the world's annual military spending. The cost of a ten-year programme to provide for essential food and health needs in developing countries is less than half of one year's military spending. Moreover, arms production is not just a matter of spending but of manpower and skills. It is profoundly disturbing to realize that in East and West a very large proportion of scientists and much of the scientific resources of the universities and industry are devoted to armaments.[1]

Increased Military Spending

Both the Soviet Union and the United States are spending vast sums for military purposes—much more than they were in 1980 when the Brandt Commission first reported. By 1984 military expenditures worldwide were greater than the total an-

---

1. Brandt Commission, *North-South, A Program for Survival.* Cambridge, Mass.: M.I.T. Press, 1980, pp. 117-118.

nual income of the poorer half of the world's people. We need to be reminded again of the words of former General Dwight D. Eisenhower spoken shortly after he became president of the United States: 'Every gun that is made, every warship launched, every rocket fired, signifies, in the final sense, a theft from those who hunger and are not fed, those who are cold and are not clothed."[2]

If most Americans feel, as I do, that capitalism with all of its faults is still a system which is superior to communism, why are Americans so dominated by the fear that communism will prevail? Instead of being paralyzed by a fear of communism, American public policy should be motivated by a desire to correct capitalism's weaknesses at home and to provide the economic aid which will enable it to be more attractive than communism to the people who live in LDCs.

How to correct capitalist weaknesses in the United States is beyond the scope of this book. Suffice it to say that it must include the provision of equal opportunities for all, regardless of sex, color, or national origin. How to make capitalism the most attractive alternative for third-world peoples has been a major theme of this book. American economic aid can promote this process.

To suggest that such a change in foreign policy be made will doubtless be considered by many to be naive. But the "realism" of a policy of pure self-interest clearly has not worked. In the poorest sections of the world, people are poorer than they were a decade ago. In the United States, self-interest has resulted in an arms race which has produced the largest budgetary deficits in the history of the country. It has also produced high interest rates, high unemployment, and the impoverishment of many smokestack industries. It is time for a change.

What Can I Do?

What can I do? This book has been written in the conviction

---

2. Address entitled "The Chance for Peace," before the American Society of Newspaper Editors, April 16, 1953.

that the first step toward the answer to this question is to become informed concerning the basic reasons for the lack of economic development in some parts of the world. We also need to know what has been done thus far to seek to solve these problems. When we have this understanding we are in a position to do our part to influence foreign policy toward the economic development of LDCs.

Visit, Listen

Problems become more vivid when reading if accompanied by personal experiences. Many of the readers of this book are in a position to take a trip to an LDC—or better still, to several LDCs. For most Americans, Mexico could be reached with the least expense, but one can with relatively little additional expense go to a country like Jamaica, Honduras or Haiti (the country with the lowest per capita GNP of any country in the Western Hemisphere). Don't be content to visit the capital city alone. Go to the rural areas. Remember that it is more appropriate that you travel as a pilgrim than as a tourist. Kosuke Koyama differentiates the two as follows: "The pilgrim treads sensitively on the holy ground; the tourist tramples on sacred sites and photographs their remnants. The pilgrim travels with humility and patience; the tourist with arrogance and in haste."[3]

Use public transportation as you go to the rural areas. In Haiti use small buses called "camion." You will find that you are packed in more tightly than you have ever been before. Some riders ride on top of the bus. Don't try that unless you have dark glasses, a straw hat, and some suntan lotion to protect you from the hot sun. If you are able to get space in the bus, you may have to share it with chickens or animals. A trip like this will show you how rough the roads are, how poor many of the homes are, and how small the gardens are which provide food. This trip will teach you much more about the poverty of an LDC than you will have learned by reading chapters 1 and 2 of this book.

---

3. *The Other Side*, vol. 22, March 1986, p. 38.

You can gain a better perspective on poverty in LDCs if you also visit some of the poverty areas in the United States. This was the experience of Senator Ernest F. Hollings of South Carolina. When he was governor of South Carolina he refused to admit that there was a hunger problem in his state. This opinion was changed as a result of a trip he took with a Catholic nun to some of the poor areas of his own city of Charleston. As a result of this and other investigations, he wrote a book *The Case Against Hunger.* The following is a graphic account of what he saw on his visit to the poor sections of Charleston:

> Before we had gone a block, I was miserable.... I began to understand ... that hunger was real, and it existed in hundreds of humans in my own home city. I saw what all America needs to see. The hungry are not able-bodied men, sitting around drunk and lazy on welfare. They are children. They are abandoned women, or the crippled, or the aged.[4]

If you are not able to travel to an LDC or visit a slum in an American city, you certainly can invite an international student or a Mennonite Central Committee trainee to your home. Learn to know as much as you can about the cultural values of the country from which he or she comes—the food, the everyday work life in the home country, and the political problems faced. We have in our foreign visitors a rich source of information which we have neglected too often. The first foreign students to come to our shores were frequently used as speakers in our churches. Now that they have been coming for 40 years we have become used to having them and have often taken their presence for granted. We have shown little genuine interest in learning from them. But they still have much to teach us.

If you can't go abroad, you should be able to visit an American Indian community. Try to find out through con-

---

4. Quoted by Arthur Simon, *Bread for the World.* Grand Rapids, Mich.: Eerdmans Publishing Co., 1984, p. 100.

versation with members of this community how it feels to be exploited by those who have confronted them with different cultural values and superior military strength and economic resources. Share the opinions you have formed with the member of Congress from your district and with a member of the Congressional Committee on Indian Affairs.

Hunger Concerns Committees

Groups of Christians should consider ways in which they can make the problems of third-world countries more vivid for their members. A Hunger Concerns Committee should be one of the standing committees in every congregation. Their continuing assignment should be to gather current information on the needs of people from third-world countries and to see that this information is brought to the attention of all members of the congregation. Some such committees have collected fruits and vegetables from the gardens of members of the congregation. These products are then sold at low prices to the poor of the local community. The products which cannot be sold are given to local agencies such as a local soup kitchen. Becoming more conscious of the poor in our own communities will not make us less conscious of worldwide needs. Rather, the joy of being a concrete part of meeting local needs will be a stimulus to generous giving for global needs.

The problem will become still more vivid for us if we would give volunteer service to a local soup kitchen. Through such an experience we will have personal accounts of people who face poverty. They will tell us why they lost their jobs and their frustration at not being able to find new work. Often children will accompany parents. This will help us learn that poverty is not just a statistic; it is the everyday burden of real people. It also will make us more conscious of our profligacy in consuming the good things of the earth.

Congregational hunger concerns committees can on occasion arrange meals which will dramatize the magnitude of the problem of global poverty and the contrasts between the abundance of North American life and the meager diets which are the lot of hundreds of millions of people we will never see.

Detailed directions for planning such meals are given in a book entitled *Hunger Awareness Dinners.*[5]

Service Assignments in the Third World

I hope that many readers of this book will be stimulated to serve in the third world. Sometimes this service can be effective even if it involves only a short-term appointment. Through such an appointment one cannot only serve; perhaps even more important, it will enhance in those who serve an awareness of the seriousness and complexity of third-world problems. Such firsthand experience will make a more profound impression than this book or any other secondhand report.

But many of the problems of third-world countries are so complex that they demand the lifetime attention of the best minds, the broadest experience, and the deepest dedication that anyone can give.

Some colleges have made international education an integral part of the general education of all students. Some are adding interdisciplinary majors in international studies. This is a good beginning. It should stimulate students to give thoughtful consideration to overseas careers.

But more specialized preparation must be given to those who are called to long-term foreign service. Postgraduate studies are essential. Small liberal arts colleges are not equipped to meet this need. Funds should be given to voluntary service agencies to provide scholarships for persons who seek adequate preparation for long-term overseas appointments requiring specialized skills.

Financial Support for Service Organizations

This all will require substantial additional funds. Colleges emphasizing international education in their undergraduate programs should receive financial support to meet the additional costs which effective programs require. The requisite scholarship funds constitute a substantial additional cost. And

---

5. Aileen Van Beilen, *Hunger Awareness Dinners.* Scottdale, Pa.: Herald Press, 1978.

obviously funds are needed to provide salaries and travel costs for those who serve overseas. The minimum allowances which are often paid short-term volunteers are not adequate to meet the needs of long-term service workers. Such workers will have their families abroad and will have to provide for the education of their children.

Voluntary service workers are currently making a significant contribution. The January-February 1986 issue of *The Other Side*[6] has a table describing the voluntary service programs of 26 North American agencies. All have a Christian relationship. Some are Protestant; some are Catholic; some are nondenominational. Those which are denominational usually accept applicants from other denominational backgrounds if they are in agreement with the principles of the sending agency. Some of the volunteers serve in disadvantaged rural and urban areas in the United States and Canada. Many of them serve overseas in LDCs.

The total number of volunteers on the field when the survey was made was 3,085. More than one-third of this number (1,115) were under the administration of three Mennonite agencies: the Mennonite Central Committee (900), Mennonite Voluntary Service of the General Conference Mennonites (120), and the voluntary service arm of the Mennonite Board of Missions (95). The 1985 official report of the Mennonite Central Committee indicated 979 volunteers working in 50 countries.

I wrote to John A. Lapp, executive secretary of the Mennonite Central Committee (a cooperative agency of Mennonite and Brethren in Christ conferences), to ask whether he could use more volunteers if adequate funds were available to finance them. His response, was as follows: "We can use more volunteers, especially people with special skills like agriculture and nursing.... We can use more money.... We have been placing more middle-aged and older people. We have modified our support system ... but not to the point where

---

6. Philip Harnden, "Doing Theology with Your Sleeves Rolled Up," *The Other Side*, vol. 22, pp. 16-28.

people can expect professional level wages."

A similar inquiry directed to Paul Gingrich, president of the Mennonite Board of Missions, brought a similar response. They have had in the past considerably more than the 95 volunteers they have at present. They are now actively seeking to expand the number. Gingrich stressed the need for volunteers capable of serving in leadership positions. Some of these should be older people who are ready for retirement from their present positions but eager to serve in a new capacity.

Gingrich has made a good point. Some Mennonite Board of Missions persons have used some of their retirement years to serve overseas. They seemed to enjoy what they were doing, and they certainly were making a significant contribution.

Numbers are important. But the quality of the service and the relationships of service workers to the people served are even more crucial. Recently William M. Alexander, a professor in the political science department of California Polytechnic State University, participated in the Philippines Learning Tour sponsored by Mennonite Central Committee. He expected this tour to help him in teaching development processes of the third world to university students. After completing the tour he wrote to the Co-Secretary for East Asia of the Mennonite Central Committee as follows:

> I have known Mennonites as a small religious community with a reputation for excellent farming. I expected the tour to consist of a number of demonstrations of improved farming practices—Mennonites patiently demonstrating their farming skills for the benefit of Filipino men and women.
>
> At first the tour baffled me; there wasn't any specific focus on farming at all. And then I was amazed. We visited poor Filipinos known to the Mennonite team. They were asked to tell us about their lives—the difficulties they encountered and how they survived.
>
> I found these Mennonites doing something very unusual; they were deliberately and carefully listening to the poor. No one listens to the poor, least of all the relatively rich development workers who have studied the problems of the poor and

are anxious to offer their planned solutions.

The careful listening of the Mennonite team is based on two fundamentals of the relations of the rich and the poor. First, only the poor can and will improve their own condition. Things done for the poor and things given to the poor are at best temporary solutions. Second, only the poor know how they can and how they will improve their condition.

The listening has real meaning; the Mennonite volunteers carefully act both in support of the poor and following the direction of the poor. Commitment in support of the poorest often leads the volunteers to simple acts of compassion. However, consistent identification with the fragile problems of the poor can and does lead the volunteers to accept the dangers inherent in the lives of the poor.

As the poor struggle to maintain a fair access to the earth's resources, they incur the wrath and the violence of the rich. Police and military under control of the rich multiply the violence.

Some protection for the volunteers is provided by their citizenship. However, in the last analysis protection from such dangers is available only in a religious faith that transcends life on earth. These Mennonites have found a practical expression of their faith working with and for the Filipino poor.

Printing this letter in this book has hopefully provided the most effective answer to the question: What can I do? Wherever we are called to serve, we can serve, by the grace of God, in the way Alexander observed Mennonite Central Committee workers at their task in the Philippines.

Some of the people who serve under the Mennonite Central Committee are not Mennonites. These people, too, are making an effective answer to the question of what can I do. But it is refreshing to see how much a small group like the Mennonites can do in fielding workers. Mennonite officials believe that they can do still more. Certainly other Christian groups could expand the number of their volunteers substantially.

I noted in chapter 7 that governments provide aid for third-world development through national programs, regional programs, and international programs. The agencies operating such programs have financial resources which dwarf those which are likely to be forthcoming to church-related voluntary agencies, even if contributions to the latter are substantially increased.

But governmental agencies need qualified personnel to make their programs effective. Some of this personnel can, of course, come from the people of the third world. Indeed, this should be one of the services former international students who received their education in the developed nations can perform.

But there is a place for first-world volunteers to serve in these governmentally funded agencies as well. Persons who view such service as not just a job but as a way of expressing their Christian compassion are in a position to make a unique contribution. They should be encouraged to do so.

Conclusion

If this book will stimulate this kind of response, it will have served a useful purpose in contributing to the development of the third world. For those persons who cannot themselves give their entire lives to serving those who live in poor countries, I hope that this book will inspire them to give sacrificially to support those who are called to serve in long-term development efforts. This giving must be substantial and it must be long-term. The "emergency" will be with us throughout the lifetime of all of the readers of this book. There must be unity of purpose between those who give their time and those who give their financial resources.

Questions for further study and discussion

1. Should we eat less in order that people in the poor countries can eat more?

2. Should we refuse to buy products which have been imported into our country by multinational firms which have produced them in LDCs on land which should rather have been used to produce food for the poor of LDCs?

3. How can we differentiate between third world peoples (and their leaders) whose anti-Americanism is based on legiti-

mate grievances against the United States and those who are blindly following a Marxist-inspired program which would seek to impoverish the United States?

4. How can we influence American public policy so that foreign aid to LDCs can be shifted from military aid to economic aid?

5. What are some of the short-term and long-term opportunities for service in LDCs by people from the developed countries? What kinds of preparation are needed for people who are called to this service?

6. How can we stimulate people in the rich countries to give throughout their life-times aid for long term development rather than occasional short-term gifts to meet emergency needs?

Suggestions
for Further Reading

P. T. Bauer, *Equality, the Third World, and Economic Delu-sion.* Cambridge, Mass.: Harvard University Press, 1981, 293 pp.

Lester R. Brown, et al., *State of the World.* Washington, D.C.: Worldwatch Institute, 1986.

Brian Griffiths, *The Creation of Wealth; A Christian's Case for Capitalism.* Downers Grove, Ill., InterVarsity Press, 1984.

W. Arthur Lewis, *Racial Conflict and Economic Development.* Cambridge, Mass.: Harvard University Press, 1985.

Jacques Loup, *Can the Third World Survive?* Baltimore, Md.: Johns Hopkins University Press, 1983.

William W. Murdoch, *The Poverty of Nations.* Baltimore, Md.: Johns Hopkins University Press, 1980.

E. Wayne Nafziger, *The Economics of Developing Countries.* Belmont, Calif.: Wadsworth Publishing Co., 1984.

World Development Reports. Published for the World Bank by Oxford University Press. The address is 16-00 Pollitt Drive, Fair Lawn, NJ 07410. The paperback edition of the 1986 REPORT has a list price of $8. Each volume has both general comments on development and a more detailed

treatment of certain aspects of development:
1978 and 1979 volumes have general treatment only.
1980—Health and education
1981—International trade and energy issues
1982—Agricultural and rural development
1983—Management in development and the role of government
1984—Population problems
1985—Foreign borrowing
1986—Agriculture: trade and pricing policies

Index

Accidental deaths, 103
Africa, 37
Africa Hall (Ethiopia), 31
African type of LDC, 36
African Development Bank, 132
Agency for International
    Development (AID), 96
Agricultural development, 69-86
    to promote industrial
    development, 106-108
Agricultural extension services, 77
Agricultural machinery in LDCs,
    78
Agricultural mission work, 82-86
Agricultural output growth, 70
Agricultural research and
    experimentation, 74
Agricultural revolution, 69
Alexander, William M., 151-152
American Indians, 147-148
Amin, president of Uganda, 40
Andean Common Market, 123
Anhui (China), proportion of males
    in population, 63

Antibiotics, 42
Appalachia, 15
Argentina
    agricultural experiment station
    in Chaco, 72
    Buenos Aires, 11
Asian Development Bank, 132
Asian type of LDC, 36
Association of South East Asian
    Nations (ASEAN), 124-125
Austerity policy of IMF, 135
Average daily calorie supply, 33

"Banana republics," 48
Bahamas, 34
Bahrain, 34
Bali, Java, 39
"Bancor," 136
Bangladesh, 25, 28
    age at marriage, 66; agricultural
    output growth, 70; child
    labor, 55; infant mortality, 55;
    population pressure, 62;
    voluntary sterilization, 65

Banks, 21
Belgium, foreign trade, 47
Berlin wall, 42
Biafra, 37
Bibliography, 154-155
Birth rates, 42-43
   reasons for high birth rates in
      LDCs
Borlaug, Norman, 75
Boycotts of multinational firms'
      exports, 141
Brain drain, 97-98
   effects in Sudan, Bangladesh,
      India, and Egypt, 97
Brandt Commission Report, 143-
   144
Brazil, 28
   distribution of income in, 47;
      industrial exports, 110; infant
      mortality, 102; primary
      education, 90; São Paulo, 44
Bread basket of Europe, 69
Bretton Woods Conference, 130,
   133
Bribery of government officials, 40
Burkino Faso, 60, 82
Burma, 28

Calcutta, 15, 32
Canada, 29, 35, 38
Capital
   ability to absorb, 112; economic
      definition of, 19, 21;
      formation, 26; human, 89
Capitalist bias, 12-133
Capitalist countries, 12, 145
Caribbean Common Market
   (CARICOM), 124
Caribbean Free Trade Association
   (CARIFTA), 124
Castro, Fidel, 118

Central American Common
   Market, 123
Children an economic asset in
   LDCs, 54-55
Chile, lack of attention to
   agriculture, 107
China, 28, 30, 34, 38
   agricultural growth, 70, 75-76,
      82; communes dismantled,
      72; foreign students in, 96;
      one-child family policy, 43,
      58, 63-64; overseas Chinese,
      40; paramedics, 103
Christian altruism, 143
Christian church, world fellowship
   of, 16
CIMMYT, 75
Cities, growth of, 44
Clausen, A. W., 131
Club of Rome, 58
Cold War, 142
Collective farms in socialist
   countries, 72
Colombia
   infant mortality, 91; years of
      mothers' schooling, 66
Colonial past in LDCs, 37-38
"Communist" countries, 12
Comparative economic systems, 12
Conscience of Christians, 15, 18
Conservatism of peasant farmers,
   78
Consumer expenditures (C), 25, 30
Contraceptives in LDCs, 57, 66, 91
Corn (maize), 76
Cost/benefit ratio, 55
Costa Rica, exports of, 48
Côte d'Ivoire, language of
   instruction, 93
Cultural values, 21, 34, 56
Customs unions, 121-125

compared with free
trade associations, 123;
political benefits, 122

Death rates, 42-43
"Deficits without tears," 135
Deforestation, 59-60
Denmark, large
public sector, 51
Development aid from rich
countries, 112
Development banks, 121
Desertification, 60-61
droughts, 61
Discussion questions, 12, 35, 51,
67-68, 86-87, 104, 120, 137-
138, 153-154
Distribution of income, 19, 34
effect of education on, 92, 97
Distribution of wealth, 34
Djibouti, 20
Domestic servants in LDCs, 45
Dropouts in elementary schools,
56-57

East African Economic
Community, 124
Eastern bloc, 12, 29, 34-35
Eating less, 140-141
Economic colonialism, 18, 38, 48,
70
Economic research in agriculture,
74
Education of mother and family
size, 66
Education, role in development,
88-101
correspondence schools, 99-100;
higher education, 95-97;
overeducate, 100; primary

education, 90-92; secondary
education, 92-95; vocational
education, 100-101, 108
Educational expenditure, 98-100
as a share of GNP, 99; benefits,
90; costs, 89, 90; buildings,
89; equipment and supplies,
90; for teachers, 89; income
distribution, 92; meeting costs
of, 98-100
Egypt, 28, 37
Eisenhower, Pres. Dwight D., 145
Elasticity of demand
"price" and "income," 49
Emergency food aid, 139-140
England, 31
nationalization of coal mines, 50
Entrepreneurship, 20
Ethiopia17, 27-28, 31, 33, 37-39
45, 56, 59
Addis Ababa, 44; Orthodox
Church, 73; Haile Selassie
University, 95; language of
instruction, 93; manure chips
used as fuel, 79
European Coal and Steel
Community, 122
European Economic Community,
82, 122-123, 125
Export dependence of LDCs, 47
Exports of industrial products, 110

Family size and income level, 65
Federal Deposit Insurance
Corporation (FDIC), 118
Fertilizer, 78-80
"Night soil," 79
Financial support for service
organizations, 149-153
Firewood shortage, 59
Food and Agricultural

Organization (FAO), 60
Foreign mines and plantations in
    LDCs, 41
Foreign trade of LDC, 47
    ratio to GNP, 47
France, 29
    Frenchman 35; large public
        sector, 50
"Fraternal" delegates from LDC
    churches, 16
Fulani, 37
Fulbright teachers, 96

Gambia, 59
General Conference Mennonites,
    150
Generalized system of preferences
    (GSP), 128-130
Genesis 1:28, 67
Ghana, 31, 37
    agricultural decline, 81-82;
        language of instruction in
        schools, 93
Gingrich, Paul, 151
Government expenditures (G), 26,
    31
Government-owned industry, 113-
    114
Government, poor in LDCs, 38-40
    lack of orderly transfer of power,
        39
Grain consumption in U.S., 140
Great Britain, 29, 37
Green Revolution, 75-77
"Greenhouse effect," 60
Grenada, 34
Gross National Product (GNP) 17,
    25
    exchange rate, 31; mathematical
        definition of, 25; moral
        judgments, 26; per capita, 25,

27-30, 34-35; weaknesses of
    GNP statistics, 30-32, 35
Gunden, Randal, 13

Haiti, 83, 146
Hamilton, Alexander, Report on
    Manufactures, 115
Hausa, 37
Health, 101-104
    hospitals, 103; sanitary facilities,
        103
High-income oil exporters, 29
Higher education, 95-97
    overemphasis on in LDCs, 95;
        University of East Africa, 96
Hollings, Senator Ernest F., 147
Honduras, exports of, 48
Hong Kong, 125
    exports of industrial products,
        110
Hunger Concern Committees, 148
    hunger-awareness dinners, 149

Ibo, 37
Iceland, 34
Illiteracy, 35
Import substitution, 17, 109
India, 15, 28, 34, 38, 70
    agricultural output growth, 70,
        75, 82; Indian (overseas), 41;
        infant mortality, 55;
        population of, 64-65; sterili-
        zation (compulsory), 65
Indonesia, 28, 39, 50
Industrial development, 105-120
    capital for 110-111; government
        intervention, 113
Industrial market economies, 29
Industrial Revolution, 42, 57, 69
Inequality in wealth and income,
    46

statistics of, 46
Infant food formula, 102-103
Infant industry protection, 115-116
Infant mortality, 32-33, 55, 102
Infrastructure, 17, 21, 108
Inter-American Development
    Bank, 132
International Bank for
    Reconstruction and
    Development
    (IBRD), (see also World Bank),
    131-132
International Commodity
    Agreements, 125-128
    sugar, 126; tin (buffer stock),
    126; wheat, 126
International Development
    Association (IDA), 131-132
International Finance Corporation
    (IFC), 132
International Labour
    Organisation, 46
International lending agencies,
    130-137
International Monetary Fund, 118,
    133-137
    "extended facility", 134;
    Kingston, Jamaica, meeting,
    137; quotas, 133-135
International Rice Research
    Institute (IRRI), 75
International students in liberal
    arts colleges, 98
Inventory accumulation, 26
Investment (I), 26, 30
Iraq, 50
Iran, 28
Ireland, Irish, 35
Irrigation, 80
Italy, 29
    Italian, 35

Jackson, Jesse, 19
Jamaica
    exports of, 48; lack of attention
        to agriculture, 107
James 2:1-4, 9, 15
Japan, 20, 29, 35
    agricultural growth, 75;
        education in, 89; government-
        owned industry, 114;
        population growth, 61;
        proportion of children in, 62
Java, child labor, 55
Jellife, Dr. Derrick, 102
Johnson, Pres. Lyndon B., 39

Katyn forest massacre, 142
Kennedy, Pres. John F., 39
Kenya, 37, 39
    distribution of income in, 47;
        infant mortality, 91;
        population growth, 61;
        primary education, 90;
        proportion of children in, 62
Keynes, John Maynard (Lord), 136
Kilimanjaro (Tanganyika), 37
Korea, South, 28
    agriculture to promote industry,
        107; Air-Correspondence
        School, 99-100; children
        provide social security, 56;
        exports of manufactures, 110;
        primary education, 90;
        schooling of mothers, 66
Koyama, Kosuke, 146
Kreider, Alan F., 13
Kreider, Evelyn B., 14

Labor, economic
    definition of, 19
Labor intensive industry, 110
Land, economic definition of, 19

Land tenure reform in Japan, 71-74
Lapp, John A., 150
Latham, Dr. Michael, 102
Latin-American debt, 117
Latin American Free Trade Association (LAFTA), 123
Latin-American type of LDC, 36
Less Developed Countries (LDCs), 11-12, 15-17, 30, 34
    heterogeneity and similarity, 36; population growth in, 42
Liberation theology, 17
Liberia, 37-38
Life expectancy at birth, 28-29, 32-33, 88, 101-102
Listening to the poor, 151-152
Literacy, 32-33, 88
Loewen, Melvin J., 13, 79
London Mennonite Centre, 13
Low-income economies, 27-28
Luxembourg, 34

MacArthur, Gen. Douglas, 71
Machismo, 56
Malaysia
    agriculture to promote industry, 107; educational expenditures, 92; exports of, 48; primary education, 90
Malthus, Thomas R., 42, 57
Marketing agricultural products, 81
Marshall Plan, 111
Marxism, 17, 141-142
    Karl Marx, 72
Masai tribe in Africa, 39
Meiji, Emperor, 89, 91
Menno Simons, 16
Mennonite Central Committee (MCC), 83

Non-Mennonites serving under MCC, 152; Philippines Learning Tour, 151; TAP (Teachers Abroad Program), 94; trainees, 147; Voluntary Service program, 150
Mexico, 28, 50
    sorghum production, 76-77
Middle-income economies, 27-28
Military dictatorships in LDCs, 39, 141
Military expenditure, 26, 31, 67, 144-145
    compared with education, 99; military aid to LDCs, 143
Missionaries from rich to poor countries, 16
    Christian schools in Japan, 91; in Africa, 94
"Mono-culture," 48
Morrill Act 1862, 100

Nafziger, E. Wayne, 11, 13, 41
Nairobi, Kenya, 11
Nepal
    labor of young children, 55; primary education, 90
New Delhi, India, 32
New International Economic Order (NIEO), 112, 133
Newly industrialized countries (NICs), 106-107
Nestlé Company, 103
Netherlands
    distribution of income in, 47; foreign trade, 47
Nigeria, 28, 41
    cocoa production, 41; language of instruction, 93; tribal peoples, 37

Nofziger, Jon, 83-86
Norway, exports of, 48

One-party civilian rule in LDCs,
39
Organization of Petroleum
Exporting Countries (OPEC),
49
Overgrazing, 61
Overvalued currencies of LDCs, 31

Pakistan, 27-28, 41
growth of wheat production, 75;
infant mortality, 55
Peace Corps, 95
Peru, distribution of income in, 47
Pesticides, 80
Philippines, 28, 59
agricultural development, 151-
152; IRRI, 75
Physical quality of life index
(PQLI), 32, 35
Poland, 29
private plots on state farms, 72
Political colonialism, 38, 70
Political parties in LDCs, 39
Population, 28-29
age at marriage, 66; growth in
LDCs, 41-42, 44, 53-67
measures to reduce
population growth, 62-67;
"population bulge," 44;
proportion of children in, 61-
62; reasons for rapid growth
in LDCs, 54-57
Poverty, 34-35
causes of, 18; in our own
communities, 148; in the
United States, 147
Preferences for exports of LDCs,
128-130

Price fluctuations of LDC exports,
49
Primary education
effect on family size, 91; noneconomic values of, 92;
reduces infant mortality, 91
Private plots in socialist countries,
72
Production, enhancing level of, 19
Protestant work ethic, 20
Public sectors small in LDCs, 50-51
Purchasing power in poor and rich
countries, 33

Qatar, 34
Quotas, 37

Radical Reformation, 16
Railroad map of Africa, 38, 48
Roman Catholic Church, 16

Saenz Pena, Argentina, 74
Sahel, 60
Saudi Arabia, 27-29
Saving, 20
private and governmental, 111
School enrollment, 33
Schuman, Maurice, 122
Secondary education, 92-95
language of instruction, 93
Seers, Dudley, 33
Selassie, Emperor Haile, 73
Self-employment in LDC, 40
"Shoe standard" of living, 33
Sichuan province of China
population policy, 63
Simon, Julian, 58
Singapore, exports of industrial
products, 110
Social overhead capital, 21
Social security

in China, 63; provided by
children in LDCs, 56
"Soft loan" window of World
Bank, 131
Somalia
decline in food production, 81
Sorghum, 76
South Africa, 28
Spain, 29
Spanish, 35
Special Drawing Rights (SDR),
134, 136
Sri Lanka, 33
age at marriage, 66; growth of
food production, 81
Stamp, Sir Dudley, 136
Standards of living, 16, 18
State farms in socialist countries, 72
"Statistical Nakedness," 30
Subsistence production, 17, 30, 40,
51
Sudan, 37
Sweden, large public sector, 51
Swiss bank accounts, 46-47
Synthetic products compete with
LDC exports, 49, 127

Taiwan, 106
agriculture to promote industry,
107
"Take off" in economic growth, 42
Tanzania (formerly Tanganyika),
37, 59
Tariffs, 37
Teacher Training Colleges (normal
schools), 93
Teachers Abroad Program (TAP),
94
Teachers for East Africa (TEA), 95
"Terms of trade," 49
deterioration of in LDCs, 50

Thailand, 28
children provide social security,
56
Third world, 12, 149
Third world debt, 116-119
ratio of debt service to exports,
117; Sudan default, 118
Tourism, 31
Treaty of Rome, 122
Tropical rain forest, 59-60
Turkey, 28
children provide social security,
56; growth of wheat
production, 76

Uganda, 40
Unemployment, 44
among educated youth, 100-
101; disguised
unemployment, 44; social
costs, 115
Union of Soviet Socialist
Republics, 29, 113
emphasis on industry at expense
of agriculture, 69, 105-106
foreign students in, 96;
lagging agricultural output,
70; private plots, 72
United Nations, 40, 112, 142
Conference on Trade and
Development (UNCTAD),
112, 128; Development
Program (UNDP), 133;
Institute for Social Studies, 33
United States, 20, 29, 33, 35, 38
distribution of income in, 46;
population growth, 61, public
sector, 113

Vaccination, 102
Vietnam, 28

Vietnam War, 142
Volta dam, 31
Voluntary service, 148
    in third world countries, 149;
        organizations, 150; through
        government agencies, 153

Wage employment in LDCs, 41
Ward, Barbara, 38
Warsaw Pact, 30, 34-35
Washington (state of), 61
Wasteful consumption of rich

nations, 67
West Germany, 29
Westchester County, N.Y., 15
World Bank, 12-13, 27, 32, 34, 41,
    43, 46, 50, 81, 131-132
World Development Reports, 12,
    27, 33-34, 54

Zaire, 13, 92
    language of instruction, 93
Zambia, lack of attention to
    agriculture, 107

The Author

Carl Kreider has given a lifetime of distinguished service both to the Mennonite Church and to higher education. Best known as the dean of Goshen College for 26 years (1944-70), he also served that institution as acting president (1950-51, 1970-71), provost (1971-72), and professor of economics since 1940. He was also dean of the College of Liberal Arts of International Christian University in Tokyo, Japan, at the time of its founding (1952-56) and visiting lecturer in economics there 1972-73. He was Fulbright Lecturer in Economics in Ethiopia in 1963-64. He was named Dean Emeritus of Goshen College in June 1985.

His scholarly articles on the international commercial policies of the United States have appeared in the *American Economic Review, American Political Science Review,* and *Southern Economic Journal.* His books include *The Anglo-American Trade Agreement* (Princeton University Press, 1943), *Helping Developing Countries* (Herald Press, 1968), and *The Christian Entrepreneur* (Herald Press, 1980).

Kreider has served on numerous community, church, and educational committees and boards. He was chairman of the Mennonite Church General Board (1973-75) and a member for nine years. He was president of the Oaklawn Psychiatric Center Board in Elkhart, Indiana, for four years and a member for nine. A member of the Overseas Committee of the Mennonite Board of Missions (1961-72), he was chairman for four years. Kreider's long-term service on the Committee on Liberal Arts of the North Central Association of Colleges resulted in his appointment in 1974 as an honorary member of the association.

Born in Wadsworth, Ohio, Kreider currently lives in Goshen, Indiana. He and his wife, Evelyn (Burkholder), are the parents of four children: Alan, Rebecca (Mrs. Weldon Pries), Stephen, and Thomas. They have three grandchildren. The Kreiders are active members of the Goshen College Mennonite Church.